I HAVE A MILLION THINGS TO DO!

real support for today's parents
in confirming their children's faith

Written by Michael and Terri Quinn
in co-operation with the Armagh diocesan
Family Ministry team

Handbook for the *'Confirming Faith in the Family'* Programme

FAMILY CARING TRUST

First published 2002
by Family Caring Trust,
8 Ashtree Enterprise Park
Newry
Co. Down
BT34 1BY
Tel. 028 3026 4174
(Fax. 028 3026 9077)
Website: familycaring.co.uk
Email: office@familycaring.co.uk

Printing: Universities Press (Belfast)

We are grateful to Veritas Publications
for permission to include prayers from
the Alive-O school programme.

ISBN 1 872253 19 9

CONTENTS

INTRODUCTION

Parents are under awful pressures today. So much comes at us. And so much has changed. Many of us are no longer sure about what is important or how things fit together. When someone talks about 'handing on faith' we may even wonder if we *have* much faith to pass on. We have not been encouraged to see our doubts and questions as something good, even *essential*. People who are searching for God and trying to make sense of life today *need* to question things.

In writing this book, the authors do not pretend to have solutions. They merely want to offer you a chance to pause amid the hectic pace of life and give yourself space to think about what you want for yourself and your family. A book (or the short course linked with it) won't sort everything out, but if it helps to give you a better sense of direction that will be great.

Who is this book aimed at?

We have written the book for ordinary parents, hoping you will find it simple and practical. It is for anyone with responsibility for parenting a child, whether you are a practising Catholic or not, and particularly if you think, "This isn't for me!" – Jesus has a special love for anyone who has a sense of being on the margins. Whatever situation you are in, however, one thing you can be sure about is that the answers *you* find will not be the same as other people's answers because families come in all shapes and sizes. So we have included many things in this book that will be suitable for some people and unsuitable for others. Please reject what does not suit you – you need feel no guilt about that. Use what helps you, and ignore the rest.

Where do the ideas come from?

The information about parenting in these pages is based on much recent research (you will find details of that research on our website at www.familycaring.co.uk), and parents usually recognise that it makes a lot of sense. Our emphasis on the holiness of daily family living, however, may be different to what some of you may have picked up as children. This is because it is part of the rich teaching of the Second Vatican Council that is only now beginning to filter through to families. Initially, some people may see this as a 'watering down of religion' because they are more comfortable with a religion of rules rather than with the love and respect for one another that Jesus preached. But we hope it will replace unnecessary guilt and will free you and your family in all sorts of ways. That is what Jesus came on earth to do.

Part of a course

The book is designed to be useful on its own to any parent who picks it up, but it is particularly effective as part of a four-session programme for parents of children preparing to make their Confirmation. (Much of it is based on the video script of the programme.) Perhaps that needs to be borne in mind, for this is not a book to be read in one go: it is probably best to leave a little time between reading each chapter. The leader's guide and video for the programme is available separately from Family Caring Trust.

Acknowledgements

We would like to thank all the people who read and commented on this book or helped to test the programme throughout the archdiocese of Armagh and beyond, particularly those who trained the first groups of facilitators, Mary Cunningham, formerly of Barnardos, and Maureen Treanor of All Hallows. Also Vera Durkin, formerly Diocesan RE Adviser to schools in Dromore, Fr Finbarr Lynch SJ, Breige O'Hare of Down and Connor Family Ministry, David Thomas of the Bethany Family Institute, and our good friends Naomi and John Lederach.

A special word of thanks is due to the Armagh diocesan family ministry team of lay people, priests, parents and teachers who gave willingly of their time and energy in dreaming up and shaping this entire project. Denis Bradley of Accord. Tony Hanna of the Family of God Community. Muireann Maguire, catechist. Fr Peter McAnenly, the Diocesan Adviser for Religious Education. Eileen McCreesh, teacher. Fr Robert McKenna and Fr Andrew McNally, the two Directors of Family Ministry during the span of the project. And Fergus McMorrow, the Diocesan Director of Youth Ministry. We are also very appreciative of the commitment of Fr Peter O'Reilly of Veritas, who took time out to read through much of this material and made valuable comments on it.

Chapter 1: What do Children Need?

Everyone was annoyed and cross with twelve-year-old Peter. He had started to smoke, had stolen money for cigarettes, and told lies in an attempt to cover up his crime and put the blame on his sister. When his sister told the truth about his stealing, he had gone looking for her later and kicked her until she could scarcely walk. Now he was grounded for two days and was in everyone's 'bad books.' Worst of all, the granny whom he adored had just arrived and had been given the whole story, blow by blow. She sent for Peter.

"Peter," she said, putting her arms around him, "My big handsome grandson! You've been having such a tough time lately. But everyone makes mistakes, and I know you've a heart of gold."

Peter melted into tears. He knew his behaviour had been awful, but this was so typical of granny to overlook things like that and believe the best of you. Granny was granny...

That is what God is like too. Someone has described God as a lousy parent who forgives you even before you say sorry and who loves the 'bad eggs' among us more than the good ones. God has more time for those of us who are in pain than for those who are sailing along without a worry. We mess up our lives – and other people's lives – and we expect God to be disappointed with us and angry. Instead, God welcomes us with open arms and says, "Peter, you have exceeded all my expectations!" We know we've messed up, and that we haven't exceeded anybody's expectations, but, like granny, God is God...

Stresses and pressures

Parents need to hear that. When Confirmation time comes around, we often feel guilty about the level of faith in our homes and feel we are messing up. All because we have such mistaken ideas of God. God is the policeman who finds fault, the judge whom we can never satisfy. Not the hen that gathers her chicks under her wings or the prodigal father who loves us ridiculously. Not the God with the twinkling eyes who wants to pour the Spirit of Love into our hearts.

It's hard to be a parent today. Life has changed a lot since we were children, and we often feel lost. It's not all change for the worse by any means, but bringing up children is maybe the toughest thing in life for most of us. Rebellious and rude behaviour is occurring at a younger and younger age. And there are more pressures than ever: we're always on the run, trying to catch up on things, and we never do seem to catch up. So we keep going, doing our best but often feeling hassled and stressed, unhappy about our family life, yet with little time to stop and think or ask what it's all about. Worries about children's faith are just another pressure, adding to our sense of guilt and of hopelessness and of not being able to measure up.

What does God expect!

Maybe the first thing we need to say to reassure you is to remind you that God does understand your circumstances and does not expect the impossible. God knows the problems you are facing, whether you are a lone parent, or you have a difficult child, or you have severe money worries, or your partner has a drink problem or whatever.

Another thing you can be reassured about: God certainly does not expect you to be running to a lot of church ceremonies or saying a lot of prayers or talking a lot of religion to your children. After all, what did Jesus ask us to do? He said, "Love one another. By this everyone will know you are my disciples if you have love one for another." He didn't say, "Pray for a half an hour every day." We'll not get too far without saying prayers, but **our real prayer lies in the way we live our daily lives and how we love one another**. Especially in our own families. That's what holiness is all about (and, as you'll see, it's also what Confirmation is all about!). You sometimes hear people say when someone dies, "He was holy – he said a lot of prayers." But they're missing the point. It would make more sense if they said, "He was holy – he loved whoever he met, especially those in his own family." I say *especially* them, because they are the hardest to love.

Gentlelove and Firmlove

Loving our families, then, is terribly important. But what does that mean? What is this love that children need?

There is a lot of agreement today that the love children need has two shapes – firmlove and gentlelove. Gentlelove is about being

7

affectionate, encouraging, listening, giving hugs... Firmlove means taking a firm stand at times and helping children to be more responsible.

Those are two basic needs of children that help them to grow up feeling secure and knowing they are loved. Gentlelove may be more important than firmlove, but there is general agreement today that a balance of the two in *some* form or other is the right approach. We can't leave either of them out.

1. Gentlelove

Let's look at gentlelove first. It's about being flexible and warm and soft – like the granny in the story above. It's about hugging children, telling them stories, chatting with them, praying together, eating together, having fun together. It means respecting children and making time to give them positive attention. And the best *time* to give positive attention is not when they are *demanding* it but when they are *not* expecting it. Gentlelove takes children by surprise, you buy them an ice cream when they're *not* whinging for it, you suggest a game of cards – or a water fight – you join them at bedtime for a chat, a story, a prayer, a hug – so it's not on demand.

Gentlelove is about being open to listening even at times that don't suit. It means getting to know the details of what's going on in our children's lives and remembering to ask about those details – not just 'How was school?' (which is a conversation stopper), but "Well, how did your match go?" (You see, you knew about the match and you remembered to ask!) "What did your teacher say about your poem?" "Was Elaine back in school today?" "How's her Mum, by the way?" It means watching some of *their* TV programmes along with them instead of leaving them on their own to watch TV or play video games. They see and hear things differently when a parent is sitting beside them. We sometimes think we have much less to give children nowadays because their computer skills may be greater than ours, but what they will never cease to need is our presence, out time for them, our love.

Part of gentlelove, too, is being a real person. Children need us to be real, to be ourselves, to not pretend, to say what we honestly feel and think and what's important to us, to be able to say, "I'm sorry"

8

when we lose the bap, and to say "I don't know" when we're not sure. In other words, to be human. They spend so much time today with TV or with their own age group and they don't have enough time with real adults, with us – which is what helps them to mature. That's the importance of spending time connecting with them.

Gentlelove is not soft or easy on *parents*. It's demanding. It asks us to spend time with our children that we'd rather spend at some sport or tidying the house, or watching TV, or working overtime. But that is what "Love one another" means. Giving up what I feel like doing for the sake of another. And an awful lot of parents are *already* doing that, putting themselves out for their children. Even when you're feeling mad with your kids and don't feel *any* affection, you still get up in the middle of the night to attend to a child and you still hang in with an uncooperative son or daughter, and you're constantly making sacrifices of time and money and energy. And that is love. In these ways you are already doing a lot to confirm your children, allowing the Holy Spirit to strengthen and build them up. So don't worry if feelings of affection aren't even there some of the time. *Feelings* of love are not the point with gentlelove – it's how we *act* that matters.

So that's gentlelove. Spending time with children and giving them positive attention, especially when they are *not* expecting it. And if they don't want a hug, it just might work if *you're* the person who needs the hug and you say, "I've had a rough day. I'd just love a hug. Ahh! It's nice to feel your arms around me. Thanks." But don't push. Remember that each child is different. So don't worry if one child hates hugs – the same one will probably love a bit of rough-and-tumble play-wrestling on the floor – that's gentlelove too, and that's where *Dad's* are brilliant. At play.

2. Firmlove

Gentlelove is more important than firmlove, but we have to balance the two. There are many parents today who give lots of gentlelove but who say their children are unmanageable. And it is not surprising, because children need the security of clear boundaries and limits as *well* as warmth and affection. So what can we say about firmlove?

9

First of all, there are times when children need to hear a firm 'no.' They need that security, even though they may react to it by telling you they hate you. Of course they're going to react and push the limits to see if you really mean what you say. Don't be fooled by that. The trouble is that we want to be popular. So we act as if the great commandment was, "Thou shalt not upset thy child." We say 'no' and then we give in. Not that we ought to be rigid or harsh. If a child asks, "Can I watch TV now?" you might nod and say, "Yes. As soon as you've your homework done." That's firm, and you haven't even said the word 'no.' But too many parents today aren't firm. They want to be liked by their kids – or they're even afraid it will frustrate them. One mother whom we met recently had two boys totally out of control and she said she didn't want to say 'no' in case it would damage them. If she could only have seen the damage that her *lack* of firmness was doing!

The second step after saying a firm 'no' is to allow children to live with consequences. Many parents find that hard. We nag or threaten or talk or even hit instead. We threaten there'll be no dessert if he doesn't eat his dinner, or no pocket money if she gets out of bed again, or no TV until homework is finished. And the children know it's just empty words. There are no consequences for misbehaviour because they know we're not going to follow through on what we say. "Ah, you couldn't let the poor child do without his dessert... Here's your dessert this time, but the next time you don't eat your dinner, you'll see what will happen!" So there's no consistent firmness and children miss out on the firm security they need. It's so much more helpful (and respectful) to give children the freedom to choose – and allow them to live with their choices. "You don't have to eat your dinner, Mark. That's okay. But if you don't eat it, you won't get dessert!" When they suffer the consequences a few times, they learn that you mean what you say. Parenting gets easier then, and *they* have the limits they need. Isn't that also how God parents us all the time? God has given us free will and the freedom to make our own choices – including poor choices – and then allows us to live with and learn from the consequences!

A third area where parents can be firmer today is in training children to do household chores. It is amazing how many parents of eleven or twelve-year-olds still make school lunches even though their children have been capable of making their own lunches for years! This is the first generation in history when most children have not had to work at home. They should at *least* have to clear up after themselves. It's good for eleven-year-olds, boys as well as girls, to have to do some of the tidying up chores in the kitchen, and to vacuum and sweep, and to start learning to cook one meal a week. If you live in a house, you need to play your part in looking after it. That's a lesson for life. Doing everything for children and overprotecting may make *us* feel good, but it doesn't help them to become responsible.

Some parents reading this may realise that they have not been firm enough. They decide things are going to change. When that change does not happen fast, they begin to nag and remind and scold. That is not firmlove. **Firmlove does not nag. Firmlove is patient and understanding, taking time to train children to do a new chore, not expecting adult standards.** It cannot be separated from gentlelove.

3. Taking care of yourself
Another thing that children need in addition to firmlove and gentlelove is to have parents who look after *themselves*. If we are overworked or depressed or drinking too much, if we don't make time for our wives/husbands/partners, if we don't take exercise, or learn to relax, or make time during the day for a snatch of prayer that helps us be aware of God in our lives, then it's likely that the balance won't be there with our children either.

We live such hectic, busy lives today that we may need to *plan* to bring a little balance into them. Some experts recommend couples to plan a weekly date – it's a great thing to get a bit of time away from the children for an evening, even just to go for a walk in the nearest park, or see a film, or go down to the local pub together for a drink. You might never have thought of that as something holy to do, something that God *wants* you to do, but one of the worst things for children is to have their parents at home fighting and rowing. One of the best things you can do for a child is to make time for each *other*. If you're a *lone* parent, you might think about how you could get your

11

mother or a godparent or someone to baby-sit and let you out now and again for a night with some friends. That's looking after yourself too. (And maybe that's part of what godparents are for!)

So. Finding a balance. Making time for each other. Taking some time out for exercise, relaxing and so on. Time to just be, to go for a walk or lie on in bed, or take a bath, or have a relaxed cup of tea. God *wants* that for you. That is partly why God wants you to have a weekly Sabbath day of rest! After all, the Holy Spirit is the Spirit of Peace and Wisdom, and we don't give the Spirit a chance to work until we clear a little space in ourselves. And part of clearing that space is taking time to pray to the Spirit for our children, especially when we have to make a decision about them or when we need to have a serious talk with them. We might pray before we act, 'Come Holy Spirit, I need your help now with this child.'

4. Faith in the home

That leads us straight into the fourth thing that children seem to need from us. They need us to confirm their faith. Think about the word Confirmation. When you confirm something, you make it definite, surer. In the same way, the sacrament of Confirmation makes your child's faith more definite, surer, stronger. But the Holy Spirit is not like the Lone Ranger. The Spirit works through us. *We* need to be working *with* the Spirit in confirming and strengthening our children, building up their confidence and their love and their faith. God works through our gentlelove and our firmlove and our care for ourselves. But how can we strengthen our children's faith if they don't see God as important to us or they never see us praying?

Now, it's true that some of us feel awkward about praying with our families. We don't know how to start or what to say. But **you don't need words. You can simply say, "Let's take a moment of silence to thank God for the food we're about to eat,"** and keep your head bowed for ten seconds. That's family prayer. And it's silent. In the same way, you might join your child at bedtime and say, "Let's take a moment to think about all the good things of today and thank God for some of them... " Then, after a short period of silence, you add "We'll think now for a few moments about the times that we didn't love, and we can say sorry in our hearts... "

12

Even seeing you pray or bless yourself helps to confirm children's faith – so a child thinks, "My parents take God seriously. They have faith." That confirms them. That's how the Holy Spirit works.

We have already said that parents do not need to *talk* a lot about God. Example speaks far louder than words. If you feel more confident after a while, however, it can help to have an occasional chat with a child. When they say, "I hate going to Mass. It's boring!" it may be no harm to admit, if it is true, "I often find it boring too. I just go because of my faith – I believe Jesus is present in a special way at Mass and in communion." In the same way, you might help your children to feel okay in talking about their doubts. "It's okay to have doubts about your faith. Some people even leave the church for a number of years. St Augustine is a good example – he lived and thought like a pagan for many years. But eventually he realised that he wasn't at peace, that nothing else could satisfy him." When you speak to children like this, you make it normal and okay for them to have doubts and to be able to talk with you about them. At the same time your own faith is coming through – though it may be years later before it affects them!

Making changes
Let's sum up. We have looked at four ways of loving our children. Gentlelove. Firmlove. Taking care of *ourselves*. And showing clear signs of faith. All are important, but each one of us is limited in the amount of love we are *able* to give. We are limited by many things, including our own life experiences, the hurts of childhood, the example we picked up in our own families, etc. There is only so much change that we are able to face. That is why the most important starting-place is probably to love and care for ourselves. So go easy on yourself. If you think it selfish and uncaring to take time for your own needs, it may be important to ask yourself where that idea came from. Very often, you will discover that it is simply a wrong message you picked up from the family in which you grew up – for example, that parents are supposed to be compulsive carers who do everything for their children and over-protect them. Once you realise where a wrong message came from, it can free you to act differently!

It is useful to plan change, but it is also important to realise that real change and conversion of the heart comes only from God. We are not alone. The Holy Spirit is within each of us – always. All we need to do is ask, even with a simple prayer like "Come, Holy Spirit... Come Holy Spirit, I'm finding it tough, and I don't know what to do. I need your support to keep on loving... Come, Holy Spirit."

At the beginning I wondered why there was so much about parenting, but I realise now that the best preparation for my child's Confirmation is to improve my parenting.

What has all this to do with Confirmation?

In this chapter we have talked more about love in the family than about Confirmation. You may be wondering what gentlelove and firmlove and taking care of ourselves has to do with the Holy Spirit coming to your child in Confirmation. But the Holy Spirit *is* the Spirit of Love. And it is we parents who *help* the Spirit to confirm our children – by how we love them. As we will see more clearly in the next chapter, the Holy Spirit does not just bounce down on the individual child but works through the whole family. We parents need to be confirming our children *along* with the Spirit. And we do that with our love.

LOOKING AHEAD: MAKING PLANS

You need space. Time for yourself. Every day. Too many parents are over-stretched, lose their sense of humour and warmth and fall back on tranquillisers, alcohol or some other escape because they haven't taken time for self-care. When you're relaxed, you can love more naturally. Your children need you to look after yourself – and to take time out with your partner if you have one! They suffer when you neglect yourself or one another. Decide which of the things below might help you cope better? When will you start doing at least one of them? Or is there another way you need to care for yourself?

- **Regularly do something you enjoy** – listen to music, go for a swim, read a magazine, go to bingo/football, take a bath, get out in the fresh air for a walk – even *with* children.
- **Talk to friends,** even on the phone – and plan to get out with them regularly. You may also need to ask them for help when you need a break.
- **When you're stressed or annoyed**, go to another room, if possible, and take time to think before you act. Try to relax and calm yourself then, and ask the Holy Spirit for guidance and strength.
- **Find skilled help** when you're feeling down – before things get worse. You might ring a Parentline (UK freephone 0808-800-2222, Irish Republic local call 1890-927277).

IF YOU HAVE A SPOUSE/PARTNER...
- **Spend 10-20 minutes each day** listening and unwinding and catching up with each other over a cuppa.
- Each weekend **plan a weekly 'date'** – even a walk together.
- Look early for skilled help when there are difficulties – contact **Accord** in Ireland, **Marriage Care** or **Relate** in Britain.

My plans for this week are... _____

_____

- It will help to strengthen the effect of the course if you read Chapter One of your book in the next few days. The chapters are written in simple language and are quite short.

Chapter 2: By their love you will know them

What makes close families?

Some months ago, we asked a number of parents to think of times when they had a sense of closeness with their families. Here are some of the things they told us.

Tinkering at the car – with my son helping. Going for a walk with my husband, even though we weren't even talking at the start. Praying at bedtime. Going out as a family to a beautiful place. Making a decision to sit down and really listen to my son. Doing some things together, even homework sometimes. Wrestling on the floor for fun. Cuddled together in bed chatting with my daughter (even though she had driven me crazy all day). When my son trusted me and told me he was being bullied, and he cried with me. After a row where we cleared the air and made up. Making a photo album – or just looking at old photos together. Walking home from Mass on Christmas Eve night. Playing a game of Scrabble together. Crying with the children the time granddad died. Hanging out around the kitchen where the 'craic' is. Putting up decorations and preparing together for Christmas. Having an unhurried meal together – with laughs and a good chat. When she was ill – I felt so close to her and realised how much I loved her. Laughing together about what went wrong on the holidays. Laying my hand on my daughter to bless her as she lay asleep in bed. Playing football in the garden with my son.

I'm sure you could add your own list of times that build a sense of closeness in the family. And it might be an idea to ask your own children, one at a time, what *they* remember as special moments of closeness. That can give us important clues about how to create closeness in future!

For 'me' or for 'us'?

But what's the big deal about closeness in the family? I mean, it's nice to feel close, but why might it be important, or what has it to do with Confirmation?

Closeness in the family is terribly important. When many of us were growing up, being 'holy' was too much about me as an individual. It was about 'me' getting to heaven, me keeping right with God, me saying my prayers and doing my duties and attending Mass and the sacraments. All good things, but something important was missing. The 'us' was missing. After all, it's not 'My Father who art in heaven.' It's 'Our Father.'

The Holy Spirit in Confirmation is not just interested in helping us to be better individual persons. The Spirit wants us to be one. To be closer families. People today are looking for spirituality in books and tapes and different kinds of meditation. They are searching for inner peace and a sense of individual well-being. Too often they *skip* family. They even want to get *away* from their families to find God. They miss the point that the God in whose image we are made is not an individual person but *three persons in love*, so I'm not much of an image of God if I'm me-centred. We're a much better reflection of three persons in love when we try to be a close family, a little 'church of the home.' That is what God wants for us.

A church?

For many people the idea that the family is a 'domestic church' means nothing. Most of us certainly don't *feel* like churches – especially if we think of a church as a building rather than people. And the word 'domestic' isn't exactly a word to turn us on today. So what does it mean that a family is a little church? Let's look at that, because it is vitally important in understanding what the Holy Spirit wants to do with us.

For at least sixteen centuries people have agreed that you can recognise a church when you see four signs – one, holy, catholic and apostolic. If we look at these signs one at a time now – but with fresh eyes – that should help us to understand how a family can be a little church.

1. What does it mean to be 'one'?

We'll start with *one*. It may be hard for some people to take in, or get used to the idea, that God wants us, not so much to be better individuals, but to be one, to be close. That was Jesus' prayer before he died. He didn't ask that we'd be wonderful at saying prayers, but "that they may be one, as you Father in me and I in you." In other words, he was praying for his church (and all of us little family-churches) that we would be like the Trinity itself, different persons, respecting each others' differences yet living in a loving unity. What might this closeness look like in a family? .

First of all, it means respecting differences. We don't have to think the same, or do things together all the time. We don't have to be so close and dependent on each other that we can't move out on our own. Closeness doesn't mean we can't disagree – some families argue and disagree about lots of things, but they're very close. In fact, we will often feel *distant* from each other, even *furious* with one another on the *path* to closeness. And that's okay. It's the *effort* we make to be close that God is looking for – in all the different painful and impossible situations in which families find themselves today. (Some people, of course, are in situations where there is just too much pain and abuse and *dis*unity: if there is serious abuse, professional help or separation may be the only answer.)

But what *does* help us to be close? Each family is different, so you have to decide what helps for *you*. Certainly, it will mean making efforts to be together *some* of the time for eating or chatting. Somehow we have to make *time* to connect with a child or a partner. Time to 'hang loose' around the kitchen and have a laugh together. Time to have a serious talk when you or somebody else *needs* to talk. Time to go to children's games (especially when a child is *not* doing well!) And it means *thinking* about one another and *praying* for each other – what is sometimes called 'carrying one another in our hearts.'

So that's the first sign of a church, the first thing that God wants for us. Oneness. Closeness. The trouble is that making time for family feels just plain boring when we'd rather watch TV or stay on at work or clean the house or get lost in some interest. So it's not easy – we won't get there on our own efforts alone. We need to pray for the strength and support of the Spirit, and open our hearts to that.

2. What do you mean by 'holy'?

Okay. That's closeness or unity in the little church of the home. The second sign or mark of a church is that it is *holy*. Unfortunately, the word 'holy' has been misunderstood a lot. For hundreds of years, families have been offered a spirituality that was not very suitable for them. It was developed by monks who were celibate, so they frowned on sex and did not see how helpful it could be for a married couple's holiness. They also had regular periods of prayer every day and thought families should have the same – which just doesn't take account of the realities of family living. The effect of their teaching is that some parents still think of holiness as being all about prayers and religious practices.

To be holy is simply to be like God. And God is Love. So holiness for a family is mainly about loving. It is back to what we were saying in chapter one – finding a balance between gentlelove firmlove and selflove. That means it is about ordinary, earthy things like sex, giving birth, breastfeeding, laughing together, shedding tears, giving hugs, wiping snotty noses... They are holy things when they are loving things. In the gospels Jesus points to the importance of the *ordinary* things like sharing your coat or giving a glass of water. That does not *exclude* prayer, of course, but it definitely includes the messiness of daily life in a family. Holy is the parent who has scarcely time to pray but who rises at half three in the morning to attend to a child. Holy is the father who comes home from work to enjoy his children, or to teach his daughter to ride a bike, or to get involved in the nitty-gritty details of negotiating pocket money, discipline and so on. Holy is the woman who refuses to be a doormat and expects the rest of the family to play their part in cooking and household chores. Sadly, we don't hear enough that this is holiness – that it's holy to teach children to mend bicycle punctures, it is holy to sit and listen to your wife, it is holy to involve children in doing chores, it is holy to have a picnic or a barbecue with them. When you soothe or hug a child, your arms and your hands are holy, for God is present then. And one of the holiest things we can do is to smile and let the more positive side of ourselves shine on our families, for God is then shining on the family too. Perhaps the holiest thing of all is to forgive. Lack of forgiveness is what kills and destroys family holiness, for God cannot enter into a hardened heart. Whereas God leaps into a family where there is forgiveness.

Holiness, then, is in the ordinary little details of daily living and loving. It includes the reality of disappointments, illnesses, failures, uncooperative children, hostility, hassle, and being stretched out of our minds. We have our good times, too, but every family comes up against failure and suffering as well. At those times, when we feel exhausted and shattered and powerless, we can seem to be so far from holiness, but we may actually be very close to Jesus. For he constantly had to cope with failure, with the bickering of his own little 'family' of disciples, even with their denial and betrayal of him. Holiness is living through all that with love, and with faith and trust in God.

3. For every kind of family

So that's two things. Closeness and holiness. The third sign of a church is catholic. It simply means 'for all,' 'for everybody.' And for every kind of family.

Some people think, "Holiness isn't for us – it's just for specially good families." That is rubbish. Where did that idea come from? Not from Jesus. It is the most unlikely families that come first for him. Traveller families, disabled families, lone parent families, cohabiting couples, poor families, fighting families, families wracked with drugs and alcohol. They're not only *included* in Christ's church: they are *especially* welcome. Two thousand years ago, the respectable people were very upset that Jesus showed special love for prostitutes and sinners, and for the poorest and most helpless people. The more needy you are as a family, the greater the sense of failure you feel, and the less 'holy' you feel, then the more you're welcome and loved and invited to be a little church. Who's to say that a little broken church isn't more special in God's eyes than one that appears to be healthy? Little churches come in all shapes.

Catholic means 'for all,' so it needs to be inclusive, meeting people wherever they are at, knowing that what helps build faith or closeness in one family may not help in another family. For example, family prayer may work well in one home, and the very mention of it may cause World War Three in another home. One family may sit down and talk things out after a row, but another family may shout and scream – and then get back to normal maybe when one person clears their throat in a particular way. That's okay too. It's the same with meals. Quite a few families never have dinner around a table. Some of them don't even have a table, and asking them to eat at a table not only doesn't work but makes them feel bad and disheartened. Their time to talk over food may be over a bite of supper in the living room – or over take-away food and a few beers. Being catholic asks us to be open to the different ways God leads us, and to see that there are as many different kinds of family holiness as there are families. So a lone-parent family needs to know that they are just as capable of being holy as a two-parent family. Because God's church is catholic, for everybody, especially for those who *know* they are needy.

Family values are realised, not only by spending more time with the family. Outreach to the poor is as essential to our identity as a Christian family as is worship. – **Parenting for Peace and Justice**

---

4. Reaching out

The fourth sign of a Christian family, of a little church, isn't a word we would use every day: apostolic. It means that we are invited to be apostles, like the first apostles. We are invited not to keep Christ's love to ourselves but to bring it to the world. The second half of Jesus' prayer 'that they may be one' is 'so that the world may believe it was you who sent me.'

To be apostolic, then, means that we are invited to think about the needs of others beyond our family and reach out to them. For most of us, that doesn't mean going off on the foreign missions. It is things we do in our own neighbourhood. Sometimes that means big things like fostering a child. Or it might be something like joining Samaritans or the Vincent de Paul Society, or training a junior football team. For some periods in a family's life, it may be impossible to do *much* outside the home, but we can always be apostolic in praying for people – even in *smiling* at them! – in visiting someone who is lonely, or in having a welcoming open house. We all know homes that seem to have the word 'private' written all over them – but we also know family homes where the children of the neighbourhood are welcome and the parents have big hearts. Such families make a real difference to the communities they live in. And that is being apostolic. It is sad that more families do not see the ways in which they are *already* a little apostolic church without even realising it. *You* may not be able to do much, but the widow's mite that you give of your time or money or energy does make God more present in your family and in the world.

What other things might ordinary families do to become more apostolic? You will know your own limits, but here are some areas to consider. Go out of your way to invite people in need to eat with you, perhaps on Sundays – an estranged cousin, an elderly aunt, a nephew with a young family. Take part in sponsored walks. Help with the local swimming club. Visit someone who is ill. Be a good neighbour, especially to an elderly person living alone or to a young family. Choose a Charity that your family will support. Recycle waste. Give a fixed percentage of wages, pocket money, etc., to the poor (if everyone in the West gave even one percent of their earnings to the poor, that would be enough to end poverty in the world!)

See if you can also involve your children in caring for the needs of others, either *with* you or without you. It will help if you are involved in the community yourself before you attempt to involve a child: 'Speak with your hands before you open your mouth' was a well-known saying of St Peter Claver. Indeed, you might talk to your children about any community work you are involved in and ask them to pray for the people concerned. It would be great if our church structures could provide more outlets for young people's idealism – more opportunities to be involved in community work and caring for others.

The need to be flexible

So those are the four marks or signs of the church. That is what the Holy Spirit wants for your family. And it is flexible: these things take different shapes in different families. In one family, being loving may mean doing *more* things for each other; in another family it may mean doing *fewer* things, even doing things that feel 'selfish' if you have been doing too much for your children all along. Similarly, some families go camping and get up early to be filled with wonder at God's glory in the dawn – while the rest of us are sleeping sound and could think of nothing worse than to be out in a field so early! Other families are great at hospitality. Other families are

22

wonderful at making music together. Others do great things for peace and justice and support Amnesty International and care about the uneven distribution of wealth in the world. So it is okay and normal and good that each family's spirituality emphasises different things.

I didn't like my work taking me away from my son, so I told him that Saturday mornings would be just for him from then on, and that I would do whatever **he** *wanted me to do on those mornings. So what did he want me to do first? Cycle seven miles to the seaside and have a picnic there! Now, this was December, and I hadn't been on a bike for years! But I got the bikes fixed up during the week, and we headed off on a cold, drizzly morning, and we ate our sandwiches in the rain. And you know something? That's fifteen years ago, and he has left home now, but he told me recently that that is one of his best childhood memories! I didn't know then that that was being 'holy.'*

Summing up
In this chapter we have looked at what the Holy Spirit wants for a family – to make it a little church. It is a wonderfully rich idea that gives great dignity to a family. But it is not a new idea – it is straight out of the documents of the Second Vatican Council and is often stressed in the writings. Unfortunately, it is a message that has been neglected and is only now beginning to filter down to families. When someone says baldly, "You are a domestic church," that may sound like jargon, or it can even make us feel guilty. We are more likely to be inspired when we see that holiness in the home is about the ordinary things, about being a warm, responsible, listening parent, that it includes disciplining children, having fun together, talking out tensions, caring about others and making a difference in our communities.

All this is not to suggest that religious practices do not have a place. What we are saying is that loving one another in the midst of the daily hassle and messy details of family living is at the *core* of holiness. St John tells us that **that is the great mark or sign of the church: notice the love they have for one another**. Too often in the past, parents were told to *pray* more with their children and it was overlooked that they needed to *play* more with them. Prayer and religious practices *also* have their place, of course, and that is what we will be looking at in the next chapter.

GETTING IN TOUCH

Below are some things that can be spiritual for a family. Tick any that you think might be spiritual or holy for you or your family:

- Teaching the children to ride bikes.
- Being affectionate, warm, gentle, good-humoured with your family.
- Firmly applying consequences.
- Having daily, uninterrupted 'space' with your partner for 10-15 minutes.
- Planning tomorrow's *family time*.
- Settling your child to bed with a chat, prayers and a blessing.
- Having a relaxed late breakfast on Saturday or Sunday mornings.
- Being involved in a choir or band or training a team, or in voluntary work for those in need.
- Keeping connected with your parents, brothers, sisters, relatives.
- Having a picnic or a barbecue.
- Attending church together.
- Sitting down together to go through a photo album – or making one!
- Making love, or being physically close and relaxed with your spouse.
- Having bedtime chats and stories.
- Hugging, touching, play-wrestling.
- Being part of a local support group of families.
- Playing cards, board games, outdoor games, with the family.
- Being real with your children about what you think, feel, value…
- Praying as a couple.
- Planning trips together, like cycling, the cinema, a nature walk…
- Doing a parenting or marriage course.
- Praying before meals.
- Being available to talk, do homework, play, listen to their music…
- Slowing down to do things *along* with a child instead of on your own – like gardening, cooking, washing the dog.
- Celebrating birthdays/ occasions.
- Watching TV or a video together.
- Welcoming neighbours/ local children.
- Treats – ice cream, chocolate, flowers, helping someone with their chore.
- Remembering the details of your child's life and asking about them.
- Being committed to recycling goods.
- Taking space and doing things *you* enjoy – for your family's sake.
- Regularly praying *for* your family – and for those in need.
- Having a weekly 'date' with your partner – a film, walk, good chat…
- Befriending an elderly couple – and maybe having them baby-sit for you.
- 'Hanging loose' around the kitchen or living room where the 'craic' is.
- Shopping, gardening, laundry…
- Talking out tensions and forgiving/ making up after a row.
- Contributing to charities/ missions.
- Having a regular weekly time to <u>plan</u> some of the things above.

LOOKING AHEAD: MAKING PLANS

Underline two things in the list above that you will do with your family this week. But don't aim too high or try to do too much.

My Plans: _____

- Take 15 minutes in the next few days to read chapter 2 – it should make things clearer – and help you to feel better about yourself!

CASE STUDY

It's nine o'clock in the evening. Dad, as a result of attending a programme for his daughter Daniela's Confirmation, has decided that he wants to be more available to his two children, spending some fun time with them. He asks them if they would like to play a game of cards, and he is open to whatever game *they* would like to play, even if it means that they have to teach him how to play it. He also realises that *enjoying* the children is more important than winning, so he has decided that he is not interested in winning the game. The children are pleased with the suggestion and the game starts. While they are playing, however, a neighbour, Joe Byrne, drops in. Dad makes him welcome and invites him to join them.

"Oh, no, no," Joe protests. "I've called at a bad time. I'll come back another time."

Everyone insists, however, that Joe should stay and play with them, so he sits down at the table and joins in the game.

Questions for discussion: *Can you see ways in which this family was a little church – with any of the four marks of the church: 1. How were they answering Jesus' prayer 'that they may be one...' 2. How was what they were doing holy – bearing in mind that God is love and anything that is loving is holy...? 3. And how were they being catholic and apostolic, i.e., including everyone, being a sign to others, reaching out to others... 4. What do you think is missing in the quality of family life today, and what difference does that make to the Church?*

Chapter 3: How can we pray when we have a million things to do?

*"Don't talk to me about religious practices in the home. We're miles away from all that. I'm not saying I'm happy about it. My faith means a lot to me and I'm sad to see the children drifting today. But life is just so hectic and pressured now. And... it's more than that – I was bored as a child by the Rosary and all the prayers that were just rhymed off, and there's no way I wanted to impose that boredom on my children. I just didn't know what to put in its place – for them **or** for myself!"*

This cry from the heart of a parent echoes what is happening for many families today. They don't feel good about the lack of prayer in their lives, but they feel inadequate and don't know where to start, even with *personal* prayer, never mind praying with their children. The result is that many parents go around feeling a bit overwhelmed by the pace of life. They carry around considerable guilt both about parenting and about the whole area of faith. As one mother said, "Pass on the faith? I can't even get the children to pass the salt!" Hopefully, then, you will find some practical suggestions in this chapter to make things easier.

A bird prays!

A first step is to broaden our idea of what prayer is. Are you aware that a tree prays? That a bird prays? That a flower prays? For they certainly do. They give glory to God just by being the tree or the bird or the flower that God created them to be. In the same way, *we* pray and give glory to God just by being loving persons – as God created us to be. In other words, to love is to pray. Daily living and loving that is in harmony with God is prayer – how you work, how you spend your spare time, how you speak to others – and about others – how you live your life for twenty-four hours a day. That is your real prayer. Thomas Merton says you pray by the way you walk or talk or even pick things up. Isn't that what Scripture means, too, when we are asked to 'pray always'? Here is a story that may help to illustrate that.

"No peace to pray!"
A father told us recently about a special moment in his life. He is
someone who goes off to a corner of the house to pray for a quarter of
an hour every evening, and on this occasion he was praying for
openness to whatever God wanted. His wife came in and told him
she had a cramp across her shoulders. "Sit down," he said, rising
from his chair, "and I'll try massaging your shoulders." Five minutes
or so later, the pain had eased and she left. He settled back to pray,
but his eight-year-old daughter burst in.

"Dad, come quick," she said, "There's a daddy-long-legs in the
bedroom and I'm scared of it." Dealing with it took quite a while
because he had to help it escape out the window and not kill it.
Eventually he got back to pray to find that his prayer time had run
out. But here is the point of the story.

"A year ago," this man said, "I would have felt angry and
frustrated that I wasn't getting any peace to pray. But here I was
getting a clear message that I was praying when I was massaging my
wife's shoulders and I was praying when I was dealing with my
daughter's fears. God is teaching me," he said, "that meeting
interruptions with love during prayer-time is an even better prayer. In
fact, I'm learning that acting with love at *any* time is a prayer because
Christ is present whenever there is love."

To love is to pray
The point he made seems to be a vital one – that prayer is not just
'saying prayers,' that **to love is to pray. And being open to
anything that helps us to be led by love is also a prayer.** Thinking
about someone with compassion. Listening to a homily at Mass.
Doing a parenting course. Having a chat with another parent about
our children. Even spending a weekend away as a couple that allows
us to come back with more energy for our children and for each other.
And it is most certainly a prayer to sit down before bedtime and say
to myself, "I've planned what I'll do for work tomorrow. Now, how
can I plan some good family time tomorrow? Mm... I'll get Joe to
help me bake an apple-tart... And I'll let him show me his new game
before bedtime..."

Sadly, there is a tendency to put religious practices into a little pigeonhole that is separate from the rest of our lives. We do not see loving our families as prayer. But St John tells us (1 John 4) that it is pointless to say, "I love you," to God unless I'm making an effort to love those around me. As we saw in chapter two, we have been misled by a spirituality developed in monasteries by monks who had regular periods of prayer every day – and thought that families should be the same! The monks did not realise that family spirituality is quite different, that to change nappies is to pray, to laugh with your family is to pray, to forgive hurtful words is to pray, to train children to cook is to pray.

Without realising it, you have already been praying a lot more than you think, and one of the goals of this book is to make you aware of that. On the last day you may be among those astonished people who say, "But we hardly had time to pray! When did we do all these things?" And Jesus will reply, "When you showed love to the least of these, you did it to me."

Times of awareness
Setting some time aside for communicating with God also has its place. If our lives are to be a greater prayer of love, it will help to become aware of God, not just at the beginning or end of a meal or at bedtime, but at moments throughout the day. As I go for a walk, I can be in touch with the beauty and freshness all around and simply be thankful to God in my heart for all that. When I'm feeling frazzled, "Help me get through this day!" can be a powerful prayer – or "I'm sorry, God, for losing my patience there. Help me to make up to him." Similarly, we often find ourselves worrying about a child and we forget to turn that worry into a prayer, "I'm worried about Martin, Lord. Please look after him. I trust in you. Thank you." The goal is to become aware of God at passing moments during the day, to be grateful, to listen, to trust, or to ask the Spirit for help.

What might help us remember to turn to God like this and allow our actions to be guided by love? Some people find it helps to begin a task at home (gardening, cooking, cleaning, even relaxing with a cuppa!) by making the sign of the cross, thinking, "Please help me to do this as an act of love to the Trinity." Other people are reminded to pray when their watch pips on the hour. Others use a pen and notebook to get in touch with their feelings and thoughts and what is really going on in their lives at present, and they find that this is a way of leading them into the presence of God. It can be helpful, too, to pray before making a decision about the children or before having a serious talk with someone in the family. Taking a moment like this to pray can help to give us the vision and energy to live our lives in harmony with God. There are no rules, of course. Whatever helps...

Recently, a mother told us about settling her son to bed. She had had a chat with him and put out the light when he said, "Mum, I'm thirsty." Now, she knew he was probably just playing for time, but she explained, "Something clicked with me at that moment, 'If you give a drink of water in my name...' And I went and got him the water." To become aware like this can be a little 'God-moment' that gives us the energy to love.

Without moments like that, it is easy to be unaware, to be led, not by love but by routine. We drift along, doing what we're used to, what suits us, what we think is expected of us, or what we can fit into a busy schedule. Without some awareness of God, we may be aware of little more than our work, the task in hand, or what's on the news or radio today. We may do good things, but it is harder for the Spirit to find a way into our hearts. When we become aware of God inviting us to love, it is easier to be led by Love.

'Me-prayer' or 'us-prayer'?

So what kind of prayer is helpful for a parent? Well, think about what we said in chapter two. We saw that the Holy Spirit in Confirmation isn't just interested in helping me to be a better individual person. The Spirit wants me to be a fuller member of the Body of Christ on earth, particularly in the little church of the home. Can you see the difference that makes? It asks me to change 'me-prayer' into 'us-prayer,' to pray and give thanks for my family – and for the wider church and the world beyond our home. Wouldn't it seem strange if a mother or father were big into meditation and 'self' prayer and neglected to pray for their family?

That does not mean that I must not pray for and about myself. Of course I need to, but perhaps not in a private, me-centred way. It is sometimes said that my task in life is not so much to get to heaven as to do my best to help my *family* get to heaven. So I'm praying to change whatever I need to change in *me* in order to be an instrument of God's love to my family and others. I'm praying to be better at gentlelove and firmlove and proper self-care. I'm asking for the grace to allow God into my life so that I become a more loving person in my family and community – so that my daily living will become a prayer of love.

The Jesus we meet
It follows from this that, when we meet Jesus in prayer, it mustn't be just someone who lived two thousand years ago but someone who is alive now, the risen Christ who also lives all around us in his Body, in our families and friends, in those we dislike and in the poor. We cannot love Jesus without his Body. When we say, "I love you," we mean something like:

"I love you in your Body – in my family and in everyone I meet. I may not *feel* any love for some of them at this moment, Jesus, but the proof that I love you is that I want to give myself for others. That is the only thing that makes sense to me. I know I don't measure up, I am proud and vain and self-centred, and I often fail to love, but that's what I want. I want to love you more than food or alcohol or leisure or comfort or work, to put your people in first place, especially those you've given to me in my own family. My heart is restless and it will never find rest until I put you, the Body of Christ, first. Please help me to love you in my family and in everyone I meet, in everyone I think about..."

That is what God wants for us. When Jesus summed up his life's work at the Last Supper, he gave us a new commandment. He did not mention loving God: he said, "Love one another just as I have loved you." He didn't need to talk about God because he knew that God is always there flowing through us as soon as we give ourselves in love to others.

Louder than words!
Maybe you expected this chapter to focus on prayer and religious practices with your children. Those have their importance too, and

we will now move on to look at them. I hope you can see, however, that rhyming off a grace before meals will make little difference in a home where there is little faith or love – or where there are no stories and little talk over the food. In your home your love and your own living faith speak louder than words. Children can learn to value prayer when they see that *you* value prayer. They can learn to love the church when they know that you love the church (which doesn't mean that you can't be critical of some things!) And they will probably learn more about Mass from the expression on your face during Mass than from any other source.

You may find that difficult to believe if you find your children reacting against Mass and prayer – "This is so weird!" Indeed, parents of older children often feel discouraged when their children abandon all practice of their faith and no longer attend church. You may then think that there is no faith left in your home. If *you*, however, have faith and trust in God, and love in your heart, then there is most certainly faith in your home – even when you feel everything else has fallen apart! Good parents have worried about their children's faith for many centuries, but we need to trust and hand them over to a loving God whose ways are not our ways!

Now, what can we say about the specifics of family prayer?

Allowing for differences

Each family has different circumstances and is at different stages, so there are many different ways for a family to pray. There is obviously a difference, for example, between the prayer of a five-year-old child and the prayer of a ten-year-old. Sometimes we forget that prayer has to keep changing. What was suitable last year will probably not suit this year. For one thing, your child may be less open to praying *with* you. Last year, you could join your son at bedtime and prayer came easily. Now he's not so sure about you invading his space. One way of respecting his privacy is to have more periods of silence. "I'll light this candle – or would you rather light it? – and we'll take a minute or two now to pray in silence for our own needs and the needs of others." (Lighting a candle or playing music draws attention to the fact that this is a special time.) Or, "let's listen in our hearts for a minute or two and hear what God seems to be saying to us tonight." Or if you like to use prayers that have been learnt by heart, you might say them more slowly as your children get older, pausing to allow time to let the prayer sink in. For example, in saying the Act of Sorrow at bedtime, *"O my God, we thank you for loving us...* (pause) *We're sorry for all our sins...* (pause) *For not loving others and not loving you...* (pause) *Help us to live like Jesus...* (pause) *And not to sin again..."* (pause) In Appendix 1 you will find a collection of common prayers.

As they enter on a new stage in their lives, they may not want to tell you what they are praying about, but they may be readier to pray more from the heart. Or they may be ready to start praying with scripture. In Appendix 2 of this book, there are a number of simple ways of using a passage of scripture for prayer with children. Some parents also like to bless their children at bedtime. Some of us have grown up thinking that only priests can bless, but *anyone* can put their hands on another person's head or shoulders and silently (or aloud) pray God's blessing on that person. An action like that can be more powerful than words. Or you can bless a child by tracing the sign of the cross on the forehead with holy water. And why not ask them to bless you too?

When you join your child for a chat and prayer at bedtime, by the way, it is good to realise that the chat is *part* of the prayer, whether you are talking about football or pop music or whatever. But it's not a bad idea to chat about your faith now and again. You might even stretch their faith a little when you let them know that washing the dishes is a prayer, that eating together, vacuuming, doing their homework, playing games, etc., are all things that, to use a human term, bring a smile to God's eyes.

Mealtimes
Many families pray before meals. It is a good habit to build – it can slow you down and help you to remember that meals are not just eat-and-run times. "Thank you for this food, God. Help us to slow down and catch up on one another during the meal. And please bless all the people in the hospital who are looking after granny and the other patients." (That is a 'little church' prayer, because it is really asking that we be one and holy as we communicate over the food, but it is

33

also catholic and apostolic in thinking of the needs of others beyond the home.) See, too, if you can introduce holding hands for the grace – it is a way of connecting, and is a sign of oneness.

It is good to vary your grace before meals, not just always saying something you know by heart. You might ask, "What are some things you'd like to thank God for before we start to eat?" You can bring the needs of others before God, including people in the news and those in crisis spots of the world – or you might mention and encourage your children to mention people who are in need of prayer. Lighting one or two candles often helps, and this is much more powerful when the lighting becomes part of your grace. For example, *"We'll light the first candle for the past – to remember all our family and friends who have died... (pause) And the second candle for the future – to put our lives and our trust in your hands, God. (pause) Amen."*

At times through the day
There are also some common situations where prayer arises naturally. When someone sneezes, people often say, "God bless you!" Those words can be empty – or they can be a prayer for that person. At the end of a phone call or a visit, we often say, "God bless!" or "Take care!" Again that can be an empty phrase – or a prayer. With the right attitude we communicate our faith to other members of the family. For example, when a child is upset we might listen and understand, but we can then remind the child, "Remember too that God is taking care of you." So God is not divorced from their daily lives or confined to a special 'prayer time.' Also, if you pray silently at the beginning of a journey, that is a way of becoming aware of God, but if you can feel free to pray *aloud*, others then *experience* your faith.

Religious objects?
We mentioned using a candle at mealtimes. Candles, pictures, statues, a holy water font, etc. do not make a Christian home, but their absence says something. A crucifix on the wall, or a picture of Jesus or Mary makes a statement about who you are. If you don't like some of the 'sugary' pictures you see for sale there are also many

good ones – or you might consider cutting out and framing attractive ones that you find in a book. Some people attach a prayer or a picture to the fridge with a magnet.

A religious object takes on new meaning, however, when you *use* it in a family ritual – turning towards a crucifix as you pray, lighting a candle as you say grace, using the font to bless the children with holy water before they go to sleep or as they leave for school... Children pick up pretty quickly whether something is an object of faith or a mere ornament. Indeed, some families have a special 'sacred space' in the home where two or more members gather and light a candle for evening prayer. There may be a picture of Mary there during May (possibly a framed Christmas card), a picture of Jesus during June, the month of the Sacred Heart, a cactus (a reminder of the desert) during Lent, and a crib during Advent and Christmas time.

The power of rituals
The church calendar offers us lots of opportunities to have family rituals, and they can be powerful ways to link prayer in the home with what is happening in the wider church. At Lent, many families make sacrifices and have one soup meal in the week in order to raise money for a 'Third World' Charity. An Advent Calendar helps to build up a sense of waiting and expecting (but not the calendars with a chocolate in each window – they have the opposite effect!) At Easter, a chocolate egg can be broken open on the table with a little ceremony, "Just as an egg breaks open to let new life out, Jesus, we break this egg as a sign of our new life in Christ – and we're now going to celebrate that by eating the chocolate!" The children will be much more aware of the chocolate than of God, but they will be happy with the jumble of Easter egg and God being all linked together in their celebration. That's how faith is planted and nourished.

Family rituals are not just for obviously 'religious' events, of course. Blowing out the candles before sharing a birthday cake with everyone, joining in the ducking for apples at Halloween, having a regular supper-time, or taking a weekly walk together in the park are little rituals that may make no reference to God, but they are certainly holy. A prayer, however, can draw our attention to this holiness. If you go out to a restaurant as a couple to celebrate your anniversary with a meal, you might say a short prayer before you eat, "Thank you, God, for blessing our marriage through the good times and bad times over the past fifteen years." (Note that family prayer is not just for the children!) You might also consider preparing a special meal with a lit candle and a prayer to celebrate an achievement, an exam passed, Mothers' Day, a Church Holy Day —or even the end of a school term (see Appendix 1 for ideas).

On the first Sunday of Advent, instead of having an 'instant crib,' we just put the empty crib on a low table. We add the straw on the second Sunday, then the animals and manger on the third Sunday, next Mary and Joseph on the fourth Sunday, and finally the baby and the shepherds on Christmas Eve night. Each time we pray, "As we prepare with Mary for Christmas, help us to open our hearts to your love, God, so that we may welcome Christ in everyone we meet. Amen."

Summing up

We hope you can see now that you are already praying more in your daily life than you may have thought —because to love is to pray. When you pray, "Come, Holy Spirit" the Spirit answers, "Certainly. Just keep on loving. I cannot work through hearts that are unforgiving, but I always work through hearts that are loving. Keep talking and listening – and hugging. Keep up the gentlelove and the firmlove – and love yourself too! Respect yourself and insist on respect for others. In that way you are opening the path for me to flow through you and your family."

We also saw that this prayer of love in our daily lives is deepened and strengthened when we become more aware of God in snatches of prayer through the day. Indeed, maybe the most important idea in the chapter is that family prayer begins with a parent's *own* prayer.

We moved on then to look at prayer with children. There is no suggestion that we need to throw out traditional prayers or religious practices, but we have tried to widen the horizon so that people in different situations can find something that works for them. We hope this chapter has helped you to feel better about what you do with your children. Remember that each family is different. In most homes, family prayer is interrupted and messy and will often feel a bit ragged. In some homes there is no family prayer, and even *talking* about it may be a no-go area: the only prayer in that home may be a silent one of blind faith and trust in a parent's heart – but that is family prayer too!

If the chapter has made you aware of new possibilities for your family, that's great, but you will never get it all together in this life. And when you're finding things tough, when life (and your family) makes you humble and aware of how little you can do without trusting in a power much greater than your own, be happy, because that humility is the great shortcut to God.

Around Christmas we 'recycle' the Christmas cards by putting one on the dinner table each day and praying for the family that sent it. You can't imagine the conversations that flow from that – memories of that family, how we met, what we know of their children, and so on.

CASE STUDY

Mary Butler joined her son Gary at bedtime. She usually found this the best time of the day for catching up on his life, for that was when he talked to her about friends and teachers, sport, television, music and so on. After the chat, she said, "I'll have to go now, so we'll just take a moment in silence to thank God for all the blessings of today." After a little silence, she said, "And we'll say sorry in our hearts for any times you can think of when we *failed* to love today…" Then she blessed him with the sign of the cross on the forehead and asked him to bless her.

*This is just one form of prayer. There is no suggestion that this is the 'right' way. But how do you feel about this form – what do you like and dislike about it. Do you see the chatting time as **part** of their prayer?*

LOOKING AHEAD: MAKING PLANS

1. It starts with you. Probably the best thing we can do for our children's prayer is to work on our *own* prayer. So the most important change many of us need to make is to become more aware of God in our daily lives. What will help you to do that? What might be suitable times for you to 'check in' with God during the day? Before getting out of bed? As you prepare food? Before you eat? As you travel to work? As you start work? As you prepare to meet your children after work? Prayer with a child will come more naturally when *you* pray more naturally during the day.

2. With your child. What will you do this week to pray with at least one member of the family? If you have done little praying with children to date, it is probably wiser to move gradually in introducing prayer in the home – you might start with a chat at bedtime and, after about a week, some silent prayer after the chat – and perhaps a blessing. When your child is used to that, you might begin to introduce a brief grace before meals. If you already do these things, you might look at the sections on prayer at the back of this book, see what you think might be helpful, and plan to use something there.

My plans for this week: _____

_____

- Please read chapter 3 before the next meeting – and look at the sections at the back of the book on praying with children.

Chapter 4: Questions about Confirmation

"I wonder how much money will I get for Confirmation?" That is the biggest question about Confirmation in the minds of many young girls and boys. And that is okay. Like the presents at Christmas, receiving Confirmation money can be all part of the excitement of a special occasion.

In the minds of parents other questions loom. *"Where will I get the money for new clothes?"* *"Will we have a meal at home, or will we go out?"* These questions are important too – there is something wonderful about the generosity of parents who want to spend their last penny on clothes and on a meal to make their child special and to celebrate with grandparents or other relatives.

This book is written, however, to help you see where Confirmation also fits into the wider picture of what you most want for your family. In this chapter, we'd like to link together all the various ideas of the course as well as dealing with some of the common questions parents ask about Confirmation.

Where does it come from?

We'll begin by looking at where the sacrament of Confirmation comes from. It all began on Pentecost Sunday. With the power of a whirlwind the Holy Spirit swept through the friends of Jesus who had gathered together in the room, sweeping aside their fears and all the things that usually block people from changing. The result was almost unbelievable. People who had been full of fear were filled with the spirit of love for others. They stopped worrying about money and security – from then on they shared what they had with others who were not as well off. People who had been running scared, worrying about what everybody else thought of them, had become a church. The church was born. That's what happens when the Holy Spirit, the love between God the Lover and God the Beloved, catches fire inside us. We don't know how many languages the apostles could speak. What we do know is that the chief language they spoke was the language of love. Everybody understands it. People who have love in their hearts don't need words. "By this will everyone know that you are my disciples, if you have love one for another."

That is the kind of loving community a family is invited to be. And that is what happens when we allow the Holy Spirit to blow through us and make us channels of God's love in our families. The little church of the home is given new life again.

Why does the Holy Spirit not have the same dramatic effect on us as on the apostles in the upper room?

There is one major difference. Preparation. The apostles had spent weeks praying earnestly for the Spirit. *And* they had spent three years close to a person who was filled and led by the Holy Spirit, Jesus himself. That was some preparation for the sacrament! But it is also a challenge to us – the best preparation a child can have is to be with people who, like Jesus, allow the Holy Spirit to lead and fill them. The best thing we can do to prepare our children for Confirmation is to bring alive our own sacrament of Confirmation. The Spirit is knocking at the door of our hearts, whispering, "Remember that *you* are confirmed. Let me bring alive that sacrament in you. Let me set fire to you and to your family. Let me heal your fears. Open yourself to me and let's both co-operate in setting fire to this beloved child of ours on her Confirmation day and throughout her entire life.

What does that mean – to co-operate with the Spirit?

That's what we've been looking at right through this course. Co-operating with the Holy Spirit means opening ourselves to being led by love. Taking seriously the command of Jesus to love one another. Can you imagine living like that for even one day at a time? You smile at shop assistants and say thanks to them. If you have a car, instead of just driving from A to B, you let waiting cars out of side roads whenever possible. You say less to your family – you listen instead and ask about their concerns and the details of their lives. You go the extra mile in your thoughtfulness to others. You surprise someone in your family with a hug, a chocolate bar – or by suggesting a game with them, something that lets them know they are more important to you than your work, that you are available to them. Those are examples of gentlelove. But you also co-operate with the

Spirit by showing firmlove and a proper degree of self-love. You say a firm 'no' when that is what is needed. You take time out to relax instead of over-working, and you encourage others to take responsibility for themselves and play their part in doing chores, etc. Those are all ways of being led by the Spirit of Love and letting your life with your family become a prayer.

For this to happen, we have seen that we also need to turn our minds to God during the day. We can make a short prayer as we get out of bed, have a meal, travel, work, relax or whatever. That helps to bring alive our own sacrament of Confirmation.

What actually happens at the ceremony of Confirmation?
The Bishop stretches out his hands over the group to be confirmed, praying to God, "Send your Holy Spirit upon them to be their helper and guide..." Then comes the anointing with oil: the bishop rests his hand on the head of the person being confirmed and makes the sign of the cross on the forehead with his thumb. At the same time, the sponsor stands behind the young person with a hand on the right shoulder. After the anointing, the bishop gives the sign of peace, saying, "Peace be with you," and the young person replies, "And also with you."

I'm not sure what you mean by 'anointing'?
To anoint simply means to rub oil on someone. For example, kings, prophets and priests were anointed in the past. The very word Christ means 'the anointed one.' At Confirmation we are anointed with chrism (a mixture of olive oil and a perfumed ointment called balsam), to share in Christ's mission as priest (worshipping God), prophet (witnessing to others by our example) and king (leading others by serving them in love).

How does the sponsor fit in?
During the Confirmation ceremony, the sponsor stands behind the young person with a hand on their right shoulder, as if to say, "The rest of us are behind you, supporting you, giving you example and encouragement."

It may be important, then, to think before choosing a sponsor. Ideally it will be the godparent (to keep the link with Baptism), but if he or she is not suitable, someone with good values and strong faith might be chosen. In the early Church, a sponsor provided a lot of support, before and afterwards, to the person being confirmed, and it would be great to see sponsors playing a more vital part in a young person's life once more.

Do people have to take a new name at Confirmation?

It is not essential: it just depends on what is done in your area. In some places, the Baptism name only is used – to emphasise the close link between Confirmation and Baptism. In other places a new name is taken, just as Abram's name was changed to Abraham and Saul's to Paul after an important spiritual event in their lives.

You might consider borrowing a book of saints' lives from the library and talking to your child about choosing the name of a saint who attracts them and can be a special patron saint for them for the rest of their lives. When they have decided on a name, see if you can find a book about the saint they have chosen – the life of a saint can be inspiring to a young person, and reading it may be an excellent preparation for Confirmation. Or you might encourage your child to think about choosing the name of a grandparent who has died and who is now a saint with a special interest in that child!

What does the bishop say to the person being confirmed?

He addresses the person, using the new name, "(Name), be sealed with the gift of the Holy Spirit," to which the young person replies, "Thanks be to God." The Spirit is called a gift because a gift is freely given, not earned. And it is given particularly to those who *ask* for it. In fact, prayer is highlighted in almost every instance of the receiving of the Holy Spirit in the New Testament. It is good, then, to build up a stronger desire in ourselves and in our children for the gift of the Spirit. A simple prayer like, "Come, Holy Spirit, open our hearts to love others" is quite suitable – or even just "Come!" Those who ask always receive the gift of the Spirit.

A LITTLE BIT OF HISTORY

In the early days of the Church, most people becoming Christians were adults, not children, and were called catechumens. Before Baptism they spent quite some time being instructed, being taught to pray and being helped to become more loving.

When they were ready, they were led down three steps (reminding them of the three days in the tomb) into the waters of a big baptismal font, often shaped like a tomb. Next – and they weren't always expecting this – their heads were ducked under the water and held there for a while. They came up spluttering and gasping for breath. (Later they were asked what that felt like, and they would say something like, "I thought I was dying!" "Exactly," the sponsor would say, "You've got it – you die with Christ in Baptism and then rise again – you'll remember that for a long time!") After being ducked three times, in the name of the Father, the Son and the Holy Spirit, the baptised person was led up out of the 'tomb' and confirmed straight away, rubbed with sweet-smelling oil just as athletes were in those days to be strengthened for a race. A white robe was then put on (as we still do with a baby at baptism) – as a sign of their new life in Christ. Finally, as if two sacraments in one day weren't enough, they were led from the vestry straight into the church where an enthusiastic crowd of other Christians greeted them warmly, and they went up during that Mass to make their First Communion. So they received three sacraments on the same day, Baptism, Confirmation and Eucharist. Note the order, by the way, because some people think that children today should receive the sacrament of Confirmation *before* they receive Communion, as they did in the early Church.

Those three sacraments together make us full members of the Body of Christ. To bring out the close connection between them, you will notice on your child's Confirmation Day that the Confirmation takes place during a Mass and includes the reception of Holy Communion and a renewal of the promises made at Baptism. That is closer to how Confirmation was celebrated in the early Church.

† only one Mass

Aren't there lots of gifts of the Spirit?
Well, the real gift *is* the Spirit of God in our hearts, but the special gifts of that Spirit are wisdom and understanding, right judgement and courage, knowledge and reverence, wonder and awe in God's presence. However, there are many, many gifts of the Spirit, as you can see in the powerful things done in Jesus. The Spirit wants to continue to do these powerful things in Jesus' Body, the Church. The Acts of the Apostles tells how the Body of Christ in the early Church did many of the same things as Jesus had done, and in every age there are wonderful examples of how the Spirit moves in the lives of the Saints – and in ordinary families! You know the Spirit is moving in your life when you see the fruits of the Spirit.

What are the fruits of the Spirit?
They are qualities you can see in people who open themselves to the Holy Spirit. St Paul lists them as love, joy, peace, patience, kindness, goodness, gentleness, faithfulness and self-control. A simple way to look at them, however, is to think of them all as love. It has been said that joy is love dancing, peace is love resting, patience is love waiting, kindness is love giving and caring, goodness is love shining through, gentleness is love acting, faithfulness is love lasting, and self-control is love respecting. Parents should not worry if they do not see these fruits of the Spirit in their children immediately: the seeds planted in Baptism and Confirmation may take a long time before they grow into strong plants that bear fruit like this. With good care, though, that growth comes eventually. If you, like Jesus, become a person filled with the Holy Spirit, you needn't worry about your children. The love in your heart and the energy of the Spirit will do its slow work of converting them, though it may take years...

You probably know the story of St Augustine. The lovely, bright, intelligent child who broke his mother's heart. He had no time for his parents' religion, he wanted to do his own thing, enjoy life, live it up. So he lived for years like a pagan. His mother Monica, like many parents today, was filled with sadness to see her child throwing his life away. She had a strong sense of failure. But she didn't despair. For years she kept praying and praying for her son. And eventually her example and her prayers won through. Augustine realised that he was not at peace, that nothing but God's love could satisfy his heart. It was then he spoke his famous words, "You have made us for yourself, God, and our hearts are restless until they rest in you." That is a lovely prayer to teach our children, even if the meaning of it does not register with them until years later.

No matter how bad things seem in your family, then, there is no point in despairing. You are not on your own. As St Monica discovered, the Holy Spirit of Love always wins through in the end.

Is taking the pledge one of the fruits of the Spirit?

In some dioceses, young people being confirmed are encouraged to take a pledge about drugs – to abstain from alcohol until they are more mature and to abstain from other drugs for life. This works best, however, when the pledge is not an automatic thing but something that is talked out. It is certainly a fruit of the Spirit when a young person knows what is involved and makes a mature decision to resist today's powerful pressures to abuse drugs.

Has there been a change of emphasis in Confirmation?

Yes. The Vatican Council has brought us closer to the spirit of the Early Church. Before the Council, people tended to see Confirmation as the sacrament of independence, helping me personally to be a stronger Christian. Today there is more understanding of the Holy Spirit's work in drawing us together in the Body of Christ, drawing us closer to our families and helping us to care for other people, especially those who are in need or on the margins of society. The gift of the Spirit, in other words, is to deepen the love between us so as to build up the little church of the home as well as the wider Church beyond the home, the Body of Christ on earth.

Is there not too much talk about love? What about fasting and self-denial – have they gone out the window?

There is nothing easy about love. It is full of self-denial and is the toughest thing in the world! Love often means giving up comforts and going against my feelings for the sake of another. It constantly asks me to take up the cross – from getting out of bed cheerfully in the morning to the hassle of settling a child who refuses to go to bed at night. Our controlled little world falls apart when we become parents and are led where we do not want to go. That is what it means to die with Christ. In the past, there was a lot of emphasis on fasting and self-denial, but there is no merit at all in suffering for the sake of suffering! Fasting and self-denial still have their place, but only when they are done out of love. The whole point of self-denial is to face up to anything that prevents us from loving others. Whenever we feel the pain of doing without something we'd like, whenever we feel frustrated, depressed, misunderstood, that is an excellent time to turn our suffering into an act of love with a prayer, "I'm feeling depressed and weary, God. Help me so that I don't punish or upset others!" In that way, you are not just fooling yourself with *feelings* of love or pious words, you are grounded in reality and can really mean what you say.

If we pray to the Spirit, are we not neglecting Jesus and the Father?

At different times in your life you may prefer to pray to one of the persons of the Trinity rather than another. That is normal, and not something to worry about. Remember, though, that we are made in the image of the Trinity (persons in love), so the greatest way to pray to God is to *be* that image – persons in love – doing our best to live more loving lives and attempting to give ourselves, like Jesus in the Eucharist, to be consumed by others.

We *do* need to get to know Jesus, of course, so that we may love and follow him, but that *is* the work of the Spirit and will certainly draw us to the Father too. In Appendix 2 and in the Resources page at the back of this book you will find suggestions for getting to know the real Jesus better.

Life's journey

In this book we have put less emphasis on the once-off event of a young person's Confirmation. Instead, we have been looking at how parents can co-operate with the Spirit in the *ongoing* confirming of their families in faith. The emphasis is on our whole journey through life rather than on the events of one day.

When a child is baptised today, the ceremony starts at the entrance of the church, moves to the book of the scriptures, then to the font, and finishes at the altar. That little 'journey' is to remind us of the journey we all take through life, beginning with entry into the Church and ending as full members of the Body of Christ, fed at the altar of the Eucharist.

For most families this will not be a journey that *feels* very spiritual. It can be hard to believe that the daily grind of working and eating and squabbling is the path to holiness. But that is family spirituality – grounded in all the messy details of ordinary daily life in the home. And that is where the Spirit moves. Through our daily loving and faith the Spirit of God gradually changes a family and forms it into a little church, a little cell of the Body of Christ whose love overflows into the world around us. Every family can make a difference in the world – in its own small way. That is the good news announced by Jesus and restated in the teachings of the Church during and since the Second Vatican Council. It can be hard to take in because we are so used to plodding through life with a sense of failure. We often feel inadequate and unspiritual and very ordinary. We can even feel overwhelmed with guilt, forgetting that we are not alone, that we have a powerful friend in the Holy Spirit whom we received in our own Baptism and Confirmation. Hopefully we now have a better sense of where that friend wants to lead us.

Summary
In this chapter, we looked at what happens in the ceremony of Confirmation and we teased out a little of what it can mean for the person being confirmed and for their family.

Maybe the most important challenge of the chapter is that if Confirmation is to be fully effective our children need *us parents* to be people who are filled and led by the Spirit. We saw that this co-operation with the Spirit invites us to be holy in our ordinary daily lives – in how we practise gentlelove, firmlove and proper self-love. To do that it is enormously helpful to turn our minds to God at times throughout the day and to ask Jesus for his Spirit of love in dealing with the chores and frustrations of daily living.

It is not easy to be a parent today. At times it may seem as if faith is almost dead in our families, and we may feel a deep sense of failure. At times like that, we can be very close to Jesus whose own life's work seemed to have failed. We can then turn to him in humility and faith and trust, remembering that our *attempt* to keep loving is all he looks for. He will take care of the rest.

When some people were walking away from Jesus, he turned to Peter and asked, "Will you also go away?" Peter's reply was, "Where else can we go?" In other words, there is nothing else in life that makes as much sense. Making money is not the answer. Or giving my life to a job. Or becoming famous. Or living to eat and drink. No matter what the media may say, there is no alternative to the search for God. We may find satisfaction for a while in other things, but only the Spirit of Jesus can bring us the peace and joy and love for which our hearts have been made.

LOOKING AHEAD: PLANS FOR THE FUTURE

1. Time to reflect and plan. It is extraordinary what can happen when we stop in our tracks, question the way we have been drifting and ask, "What do I really want for my family life?" One good way to reflect that we encourage you to use is to take ten minutes now and again to read a section of this book. It is a book that you will get much more out of when you go back over a section or a chapter from time to time – and when you *use* the prayer sections at the back.

2. Weekly planning time. Can you also decide on a regular time that might suit you for planning for your family in future? For example, a weekly planning time can include:

- Planning to take care of yourself as a person (including planning to build up the habit of praying at key moments through the day).
- Making time for yourselves as a couple on a daily and weekly basis (or with your friends/wider family, if you are not a couple).
- Planning to set aside time to make good connections with your children, having fun, listening, being real with them about yourself, and praying with them.

3. Doing a further course. Doing a short course on parenting or marriage support may be one of the holiest things a parent can do. There are parenting courses available in many areas today.

My plans for the future are: _____

A time that would suit me for weekly planning is: _____

- Take fifteen minutes in the next few days to read chapter 4 – it should help you to have a better grasp of the sacrament of Confirmation and how it fits into your family life.

CASE STUDY

"Nicole, how many times do I have to tell you it's bedtime!"

"I said I was going to bed – now will you stop pestering me! I'm going as soon as I finish this!"

"Look, you were finishing it an hour ago. You're no further on!"

"How can I finish it with you nagging! Shut up, will you!"

The voices had been rising, but Nicole's mum was now shouting.

"Don't you tell me to shut up! I'm not taking any more! Now, go to bed! GO TO BED! NOW! NOW!!!"

"NO!!! PISS OFF AND LEAVE ME ALONE!"

This was a typical scene in the Doran's home – until Nicole's mum, Stephanie attended the first night of the programme in preparation for her daughter's Confirmation. What hit her on that evening was that she had allowed the tension about bedtime to take over and to poison the atmosphere at home – there was now little or no *Gentlelove* between herself and her daughter. She could also see that all the unpleasantness was pointless: Nicole still didn't go to bed on time! When Stephanie arrived home that evening, it was past Nicole's bedtime, but she was still up. Instead of nagging, however, Stephanie decided she would talk about the bedtime issue at a quieter time when Firmlove could work better, and she said,

"Hi. How was your evening?"

"Mm. Okay, I suppose."

"Why don't we have something nice for supper?"

"Huh? Like what?"

"Oh, I don't know. I just want to switch off tonight. I'll play you a game of draughts or something – we haven't done that in ages."

"There's a good programme on – would you watch it?"

"Yeah, okay. But let's decide about supper first..."

What was wrong with the mum's approach in the first scene? What do you think of her new approach? If you had to choose between getting your son/daughter to bed on time and getting on well with them, which would you choose, and why? What has all this to do with confirming your child's faith?

APPENDIX 1: PRAYING WITH CHILDREN

PRAYING AT BEDTIME

The two most popular times for praying in the home are at bedtime and before meals. For mealtimes, lighting a candle can help – see the section 'Using Two Candles' at the end of this appendix.

There are many ways of praying at bedtime, and there is no need to change your own way as long as it seems to work for you. But as children become more self-conscious and 'private' here is one suggestion which you might consider using or adapting:

You join a child for a chat at bedtime. Enjoy the chat – it is an act of love so it is part of your prayer. After the chat, say

"We'll just take a moment in silence to thank God for all the blessings of today." (Silence for a short period.)

"And we'll say sorry in our hearts for any times we can think of when we *failed* to love today..." (Again, silence for a short period)

Finally, you dip your finger in holy water, trace the sign of the cross on your child's forehead, and say,

"God bless you and keep you safe always."

This doesn't have to take much time (though the chat will not always be short – bedtime is often the best time for a chat, when your son or daughter may want to hold on to you a little longer). You are also respecting their privacy, and it is a sign of your faith which they may remember for many years to come. With time, you can make the period of silence longer or vary the prayer in other ways (for example, you might say aloud what you want to thank God for, or mention something you did during the day that you want to say sorry to God for). And you might ask your child to bless *you*.

There is nothing magic about holy water, of course – you can explain to your child that blessing with holy water is a reminder of our life in Christ through Baptism – and it is also a sacramental of the Church. Indeed, a good Confirmation gift might be an attractive holy water font for your child's bedroom. You will need to remember to keep it topped up and you might encourage your child to use it first thing in the morning and last thing at night.

SET PRAYERS

Many of the prayers on the next pages are prayers that your children have learned at school and may have said a little mechanically up to now, without much thought. Encourage them to say these prayers more slowly now that they are older, so that they can reflect on what they are saying and deepen their faith. If you are praying some of them with your children at bedtime or before meals, you might also say them more slowly and thoughtfully.

The Sign of the Cross
In the name of the Father, and of the Son, and of the Holy Spirit. Amen.
(St Augustine also has a beautiful version of the Sign of the Cross: In the name of the Lover, and of the Beloved, and of the Spirit of Love between them. Amen.)

Our Father
Our Father, who art in heaven,
Hallowed be thy name.
Thy kingdom come;
Thy will be done on earth as it is in heaven.
Give us this day our daily bread,
And forgive us our trespasses,
As we forgive those who trespass against us,
And lead us not into temptation,
But deliver us from evil. Amen

Acts of Faith
You are the Christ, The Son of the living God.
  My Lord and my God.
  Lord, I believe. Increase my faith.

Hail Mary
Hail Mary, full of grace,
The Lord is with you.
Blessed are you among women,
And blessed is the fruit of your womb, Jesus.
Holy Mary, Mother of God,
Pray for us sinners,
Now and at the hour of our death, Amen.

Morning Prayer
Father in heaven, you love me,
You're with me night and day.
I want to love you always in all I do and say.
I'll try to please you, Father.
Bless me through the day.
Amen.

Night Prayer
God our Father, I come to say
Thank you for your love today.
Thank you for my family
And all the friends you give to me.
Guard me in the dark of night
and in the morning send your light.
Amen.

Act of Hope

Deliver us, Lord, from every evil and grant us peace in our day, as we wait in joyful hope for the coming of our saviour, Jesus Christ.

Act of Charity

O my God, I love you with all my heart, with all my soul, and with all my strength.
Lord, increase our love and help us to love one another. Amen.

Prayers to the Holy Spirit

Holy Spirit, I want to do what is right. Please help me.
Holy Spirit, I want to live like Jesus. Please guide me.
Holy Spirit, I want to pray like Jesus. Please teach me. Amen.

Come, Holy Spirit, fill the hearts of your faithful and kindle in us the fire of your love.

Prayers to the Trinity

Glory be to the Father, and to the Son, and to the Holy Spirit;
As it was in the beginning,
Is now, and ever shall be,
World without end.
Amen.

Praise to the Father. Praise to the Son. Praise to the Spirit.
The three in one.
Amen.

Prayers to Mary

Mary, Mother of Jesus, I want to live and love like you. I want to love the Father. I want to love like Jesus. Amen

Hail, Holy Queen

Hail, holy Queen, Mother of mercy; Hail our life, Our sweetness and our hope. To you we cry, poor banished children of Eve; to you we send up our sighs, mourning and weeping in this valley of tears. Turn then, most gracious advocate, your eyes of mercy towards us; and after this our exile, show to us the blessed fruit of your womb, Jesus. O clement, O loving, O sweet Virgin Mary. Pray for us, O holy Mother of God, That we may be made worthy of the promises of Christ. Amen.

Memorare

Remember, O most gracious Virgin Mary, that never was it known that anyone who fled to your protection, implored your help or sought your intercession was left unaided. Inspired with this confidence, I fly to you, O Virgin of Virgins, my Mother. To you I come, before you I stand, sinful and sorrowful. O Mother of the Word incarnate, do not reject my petitions, but graciously hear and answer them. Amen.

Magnificat *(German version)*

My soul glorifies you, God, and my spirit finds its joy in you, my Saviour. For you have blessed me lavishly and make me ready to respond. You shatter my little world and let me be poor before you. You take from me all my plans and give me more than I can hope for or ask or even imagine. You give me opportunities and the ability to be free and to burst through my boundaries. You give me the courage to be daring, to trust in you alone, for you show yourself as the ever greater one in my life. You have taught me that it is in being servant that it becomes possible for me to allow God's Kingdom to break through here and now. Amen

Mysteries of the Rosary

Joyful Mysteries: The Annunciation, The Visitation, The birth of Jesus, The Presentation in the Temple, The Finding in the Temple,
Sorrowful Mysteries The Agony in the Garden. The Scourging at the Pillar. The Crowning with thorns. The Carrying of the Cross. The Crucifixion.
Glorious Mysteries. The Resurrection, The Ascension, The Coming of the Holy Spirit, The Asumption of Mary into Heaven. The Coronation.

St Patrick's Breastplate (Prayer to Jesus)

Christ be with me,
Christ be beside me,
Christ be before me,
Christ be behind me,
Christ be at my right hand,
Christ be at my left hand,
Christ be with me everywhere I go,
Christ be my friend for ever and ever. Amen.

Journey Prayer

Arise with me in the morning. Travel with me through each day. Welcome me on my arrival. God, be with me all the way. Amen.

Aspirational Verses

Jesus, have mercy on me a sinner.

My God and my all.

The people who walked in darkness have seen a great light. God, bless with your great light all those who walk in darkness this night. Amen.

Lord, be a guiding light above me, be a warm welcome ahead of me, today, tomorrow and forever. Amen.

May the love, the strength and the Spirit of God be with us all, now, and forever. Amen.

You have made us for yourself, Lord, and our hearts are restless until they rest in you.

PAIDREACHA AS GAEILGE

An Phaidir

Ar nAthair atá ar neamh,
Go naofar d'ainm,
Go dtaga do ríocht,
Go ndéantar do thoil ar an
talamh mar a dhéantar ar
neamh.
Ar n-arán laethúil tabhair dúinn
inniu, Agus maith dúinn ár
bhfiacha, mar a mhaithimidne
dár bhféichiúna féin,
Agus ná lig sinn I gcathú,
Ach saor sinn ó olc. Aiméan.

Failte an Aingil

Sé do bheatha, a Mhuire,
Atá lán de ghrásta,
Tá an Tiarna leat.
Is beannaithe thú idir mná,
Agus is beannaithe toradh do
bhroinne, Iosa.
A Naomh Mhuire, a mháthair
Dé, Guigh orainn, na peacaigh,
Anois agus ar uair ár mbáis.
Aiméan.

Glóir don Athair

Glóir don Athair,
Agus don Mhac,
Agus don Spiorad Naomh;
Mar a bhí ó thús,
Mar atá anois,
Agus mar a bhéas go brách,
Le saol na saol.
Aiméan.

Altú roimh Bhia

Beannacht ó Dhia orainne atá ag
suí chun boird le chéile.
Beannacht ar an mbia a ithimid
inniu. Beannacht ar na lámha a
d'ullmhaigh dúinn é.
Beannacht ó Dhia dílis orainn
féin. Aiméan.

Altú I ndiaidh Bia

Go raibh maith agat, a Dhia,
mar is tú a thug bia dúinn.
Go raibh maith agat, a Dhia,
mar is tú a thug cairde dúinn.
Go rabih maith agat, a Dhia,
mar is tú a thug gach rud dúinn.
Go raibh maith agat, a Dhia.
Aiméan.

Paidir na Maidine

A Dhia, tá grá agat dom.
Bíonn tú liom de lá is d'oíche.
Ba mhaith liom grá a thabhairt
duit gach nóiméad den lá.
Ba mhaith liom tú a shásamh.
A athair, cabhraigh liom.
Aiméan.

Paidir na hOíche

A Dhia, a Athair, molaim thú
As ucht do chineáltais liom
inniu.
As ucht mo chairde molaim thú,
Agus as an teaghlach a thug tú
dom.
I ndorchadas na hoíche cosain
mé, solas na maidine go bhfeice
mé. Aiméan.

USING TWO CANDLES

We create a prayerful atmosphere and a sense of peace and calm when we light a candle as part of a grace before meals. Many occasions also call for the lighting of *two* candles, one for the past and one for the future. New Year's Eve. New Year's Day. The beginning of spring – and of each of the seasons. The end of a school term. The beginning or end of a holiday. The passing of an examination. A child leaving home. A birthday. An anniversary... As we light the candle for the past, we might offer a prayer of thanks for the blessings linked with that occasion (and sometimes sorrow for our neglect). As we light the second candle, we might look to the future with a prayer trusting ourselves into God's hands – and perhaps asking for a new, more generous spirit.

There are also a number of *times in the Church calendar* when we can add a sense of occasion to a meal by lighting a candle for the past we are leaving behind and a candle for the new season we are welcoming. All Souls' Day, Easter, Christmas, the beginning of Lent and of Advent. For All Soul's Day, for example, we might light the candle for the past as we remember friends and family who have died – and the candle for the future as we pray *with* those souls that we will live more loving Christian lives.

For all these occasions we can change an ordinary meal into a celebration by having something like crisps and dip for a starter and an ice cream to finish – or something healthier! As far as the children are concerned, the meal itself may be much more important than the candle or the prayer, but faith is more likely to be 'caught' when it is linked with enjoyable times.

Here is a short reflection, based on a well-known scripture passage, which might also be read on some of these occasions:

For everything there is a season and a time under heaven.
There is a time for sowing seeds and a time for gathering.
A time for Lent and a time for Easter.
A time for summer and a time for snow.
A time for school to start and a time for it to finish
A time for tears and a time for giving thanks
Let us take time, dear God, to celebrate you in all these times of our lives together. Amen

APPENDIX 2: USING GUIDED MEDITATIONS WITH YOUR CHILDREN

INTRODUCTION

The purpose of the guided meditations below is to help children experience the presence of Jesus in scripture. (It is often overlooked that Jesus is present not only in the bread and wine at Mass but also in the priest and people, the Body of Christ around us – and in the Scriptures.)

These meditations have all been tried by parents with their children and it is now clear that this type of prayer certainly satisfies a hunger in many young people. Don't think of them as something to be used only once. The same meditation can be used a number of times and the children's experience of it will tend to be different each time.

When to use them

Some parents ask if there is a suitable time to ease a young person into praying with scripture like this, but there is no set time. It may help to try doing a meditation on your own first: you should then feel more confident in introducing it to your children.

You may like to do one of these meditations for family prayer at a weekend. Or when a child is ill some Sunday, you might say, "You're obviously feeling too unwell to go to church today. We'll have a guided meditation instead. That will be easier for you."

There is something to be said for starting with just one child, as the presence of another can change the atmosphere – sitting in silence in the presence of each other may seem strange and can sometimes cause giggling. But once a family is used to this form of prayer they relax and the presence of a number of people can actually add to the whole experience.

How they work

Each meditation begins with a short period of quietening down followed by the lighting of a candle as a sign of the presence of Christ (the Light of the World) where two or more are praying together. It may help to put a marker at the 'Quietening Down' page below (p. 59) and at the passage you have chosen. Soft background music can be played throughout the quietening time – and through the entire meditation –

because music often creates a better atmosphere for prayer, especially for people who are uncomfortable with silence.

After the quietening down exercise, you slowly read the guided meditation you have chosen, with pauses of 5-20 seconds where pauses are shown. The suggested times are only for families who are not used to praying like this – ideally, you would need a much longer silence. It would be normal to extend times of silence as your children get *used* to them – and if they seem ready for more.

Finally, everyone opens their eyes again and you can ask your child(ren) some of the suggested questions that you think are suitable. This sharing of what happened for each one can add to and deepen the whole experience.

The suggested sequence, then, is:

1. Read quietening down exercise and light one or two candles.
2. Slowly read the scripture passage and the script that follows it.
3. Ask some of the suggested questions

Making up your own meditations
When you have led your children through a number of meditations with scripture, you might consider making up your own meditations. Pray to the Spirit to help you, then choose a passage of scripture and try praying with it yourself first, using your imagination to recreate the scene. Remember that **the goal is not to sort out your problems but to meet Jesus** – keep focused on that. (A simple book on praying with scripture is "Enjoy Praying," available from Family Caring Trust, Ashtree Enterprise Park, Newry BT34 1BY. It costs £7.95/€10.80 including postage and packing.) After praying on a passage, you might then make a few notes to help you introduce the passage to your children. You can use the same quietening exercises as are in this book, and similar questions for afterwards.

Checklist
This book – with markers at the right pages. A tape or CD of reflective instrumental music. A CD or tape player. A candle. Matches. A reading light (if you are reading these notes in semi-darkness – which may help to create a better atmosphere and cut down on distractions).

QUIETENING DOWN

The following passage can be read slowly before each meditation, but feel free to shorten or change it or leave it out as you think fit.

First, we'll take a moment to calm ourselves. It's good to keep your back straight, put your feet on the ground, close your eyes, and take a little while to still yourself first. Try to breathe through your nose and become aware of the cool breath as it enters through your nose.. (pause) and the warm breath as you breathe out.. (pause).

Now, the Holy Spirit is within you. So relax and soften your body to let the Spirit flow through you.. Your feet first, don't move them, but let a soft feeling flow through them as you become aware of your toes.. the soles of your feet.. your heels.. your ankles... Let that softness flow up through your legs into your knees – let the tension go in your knees.. your thighs.. your stomach.. your lower back.. your waist.. Now the entire lower part of your body... Get away from the thoughts that buzz through your mind, and just be aware of your body, because we can shut God out when we don't have some silence and some body-awareness in our lives.

And now let the Spirit move through the upper part of your body as you let that softness and relaxation move through your upper back.. your chest.. your shoulders. Let the tension in your shoulders go. And now soften your neck.. and the back of your head.. the top of your head.. your face. Notice the tension in your jaws and chin as you let it go.. Back to your shoulders now.. and down your upper arms into your elbows.. your forearms.. your wrists.. your hands.. your fingers and thumbs. Now relax your whole body and mind and let the Spirit of Peace flow through you as you come more fully into the presence of God.

(Lighting a candle) Jesus, you promised that where two or more were gathered in your name, you would be in our midst, so we believe you are present now. We ask the Holy Spirit to help us meet you as the passage is read... (Pause. Then read the chosen passage.)

QUESTIONS AFTER THE MEDITATION

You can open your eyes now and come back gradually to the room. Was the quietening time too long or too short? Was it hard to imagine the scene? What did you see that filled in the scene for you? Could you put *yourself* into the story? Were you able to meet Jesus? How do you feel now at the end of the meditation?

JESUS IN THE UPPER ROOM
John 20, 19-22

Many of us think of the Gospels as something that happened two thousand years ago. We can easily miss the point that the risen Jesus is present to us right now whenever the Gospel is read. The passage we're going to listen to is about Jesus appearing to his friends in the upper room. So it's good to remember that *you're* **one of his friends and to pray now that Jesus will be present to** *us* **as we relax and close our eyes while the passage is being read.**

When it was evening on that day, the first day of the week, and the doors of the house where the disciples had met were locked for fear of the Jews, Jesus came and stood among them and said, "Peace be with you." After he said this, he showed them his hands and his side. Then the disciples rejoiced when they saw the Lord. Jesus said to them again, "Peace be with you. As the Father has sent me, so I send you." When he had said this, he breathed on them and said to them, "Receive the Holy Spirit." (pause)

We'll take the first part again. *It was evening on that day, the first day of the week, and the doors of the house where the disciples had met were locked for fear of the Jews.* **I wonder can you imagine that** *you* **are in the upper room where the disciples are. Look around in your mind's eye and see the bare walls...** (pause.) **Notice the big wooden door – firmly closed with wooden bars across it, blocking the way in for fear of the Jews...** (pause.) **Look around at the disciples now and see the fear in their eyes – they're wondering if they're going to be attacked next...** (pause.) **It might be good to ask yourself what's** *your* **locked door – what fears are blocking you from letting Jesus into your life? Is it the fear of change? Or the fear of what someone else might think? Or is it just the distractions and busy-ness of daily living that lock out Jesus? What's your locked door...?** (pause.) **We pray for the grace to open it and let Jesus in...**

We'll continue with the reading: *Jesus came and stood among them and said, "Peace be with you." After he said this, he showed them his hands and his side.* **Become aware of Jesus now, and his presence to you. Sense his presence...** (pause) **Look at his hands and see the wounds...** (pause) **Remember that he is really and truly present – it's not just something we're imagining – and let him say to you personally, "Peace be with you..."** (pause.)

60

And we'll continue again with the reading: *Then the disciples rejoiced when they saw the Lord. Jesus said to them again, "Peace be with you. As the Father has sent me, so I send you." When he had said this, he breathed on them and said to them "Receive the Holy Spirit"* **Let Jesus say those words to you personally now. It doesn't matter if you can't see his face. Hear him speak, and let the words into your heart: Peace be with you. I'm saying** *peace be with you* **a second time, he says, because I so much want peace for you and for your family and friends... (pause) Peace... (pause) Trust in me and let my peace into your heart. Don't worry about anything – life may be difficult at times, but I will always be with you, loving you... (pause) Trust in me and be at peace... (pause) As the Father sent me, so I send you to bring my peace and love and joy to your family and to all you meet... (pause) So I breathe on you now and say: "Receive the Holy Spirit." I have given you my Spirit in Baptism and I give it more fully in Confirmation, and I continue to give you my Spirit. Have faith and trust in me and pray often to the Spirit... (pause) Once again I breathe on you and say, Receive the Holy Spirit for yourself and your family, and be at peace... (pause) And you can open your eyes now and come back gradually to the room.**

THE COMING OF THE HOLY SPIRIT AT PENTECOST
Acts 2, 1-4

You remember that Jesus had promised a powerful filling with the Holy Spirit, so the apostles and Mary and others had been praying and preparing for this gift for some time. Here's the story of Pentecost from the first reading for Pentecost Sunday:
When the day of Pentecost had come, they were all together in one place. And suddenly from heaven there came a sound like the rush of a violent wind, and it filled the entire house where they were sitting. Divided tongues, as of fire, appeared among them, and a tongue rested on each of them. All of them were filled with the Holy Spirit and began to speak in other languages, as the Spirit gave them ability.

Now we'll take the passage bit by bit, remembering that what is described when Scripture is read truly happens again for anyone with an open heart. (brief pause) *When the day of Pentecost had come, they were all together in one place. And suddenly from heaven there came a sound like the rush of a violent wind, and it filled the entire house where they were sitting.*

61

You may like to put yourself in the room with the disciples now and to pray for the grace to be open to receive the Spirit... (10 seconds) Can you imagine now the sound of this powerful wind, like a tornado or a great whirlwind...? (brief pause) That is how much we are loved – there is no limit to the generosity of God. God rushes into a heart that is open like a powerful whirlwind. And that whirlwind of love is here now, rushing in to fill the empty spaces in our hearts whenever we empty them of the desires that usually fill them, whenever we come humbly before God and admit our emptiness and weakness... (5 secs) Allow that whirlwind of love to enter into you now... (5 secs)

And we'll take the next line now. *Divided tongues, as of fire, appeared among them, and a tongue rested on each of them.* Can you imagine that – fire entering the room? Fire is something a bit scary. It hurts. It burns. And when we open ourselves to love, we open ourselves to being burnt, to discomfort, to putting ourselves out, going against our feelings. Listening when we want to argue instead. Being open to love means being led at times where we'd rather not go... (brief pause) The fire separates now and comes to rest on the head of each one in the room. Can you open yourself to this fire of love, to being burnt? When you're ready, invite the Spirit, who is a flame of love, into your heart... (10 secs)

And now the next line. *All of them were filled with the Holy Spirit and began to speak in other languages, as the Spirit gave them ability.* We don't know how many languages the apostles spoke when the Spirit filled them. But we do know that there's one language everyone understands – the language of love. And the same passage goes on to describe the extraordinary love shown by the early Christians after receiving the Spirit. The proof that the Spirit is alive and active in us is that we love one another – in our thoughts and words and deeds. So we might ask the Spirit now for a true change of heart – that each of us will be prepared to pay the price, whatever it costs, to be a kinder and more loving person with our families and in our neighbourhoods. If you ask for that grace, it will certainly be granted (10 secs) And relax and allow the Holy Spirit of Love to flow into your heart. (10 secs)

And as usual before we finish a time of prayer, we might take a few moments to say thanks. Whether you sensed the presence of the Spirit or not, there is no doubt that the Spirit was present, blessing you and your family. (pause) **You can open your eyes now and come back in your own time to the room we're in…**

CURE OF THE BLIND MAN
(Mark 8 22-26)

They came to Bethsaida. Some people brought a blind man to him and begged him to touch him. He took the blind man by the hand and led him out of the village; and when he had put saliva on his eyes and laid his hands on him, he asked him, "Can you see anything?" And the man looked up and said, "I can see people, but they look like trees, walking." Then Jesus laid his hands on his eyes again: and he looked intently and his sight was restored, and he saw everything clearly. Then he sent him away to his home, saying, "Do not even go into the village."

We'll take the first part. *They came to Bethsaida. Some people brought a blind man to him and begged him to touch him. (pause)* **So we'll start by imagining that we happen to be in the little village of Bethsaida that day…** *(pause)* **It's a poor village, with hot, dusty streets, no footpaths, just a dirt path through the houses. Can you see that?** *(pause)* **And now see the blind beggar being taken round the corner to meet Jesus. Can you see the old ragged clothes the man is wearing…?** *(pause)* **Look at Jesus as they bring the blind man to him. Look at Jesus' face…** *(pause)* **What feelings can you see in his eyes…?** *(pause)*

And back to the passage. *He took the blind man by the hand and led him out of the village.* **See Jesus putting out his hand and taking this poor man's hand.** *(pause)* **Look at them walking together, hand in hand, out of the village…** *(pause)*

Back to the passage. *When he had put saliva on his eyes and laid his hands on him, he asked him, "Can you see anything?" And the man looked up and said, "I can see people, but they look like trees, walking."* **Watch him put the spittle on the eyes…** (pause) **Now laying his hands on the man's head. What do you see in Jesus' face?** (pause) **Imagine what it was like for the blind man. He wasn't blind from birth – he knew what trees looked like, but he could only see rough blurred images, moving around…**

Then Jesus laid his hands on his eyes again: and he looked intently and his sight was restored, and he saw everything clearly. Then he sent him away to his home, saying, "Do not even go into the village." **Watch while Jesus with great tenderness and faith touches the man again…**

63

(pause) Sense the great power of God that flows through him into the blind man... *(pause)* Imagine the blurred shapes the man sees becoming clear now, like putting on new glasses and you can see everything like new, the colours, the light, the clear vision... *(pause)*

Now, remember that what happened in the gospels is happening right here and now in this present moment. You are no longer an observer outside the scene. You are the blind man. And there are many ways in which we all live in blindness, when we do not see God in our lives and when we cannot see the people we meet with God's eyes. We are blind to the most important things in life. Let's take a minute to be aware of how we are blind in ways that we live. *(pause)*

Now you hear people coming down the street. Someone says, "Jesus is close by." And you change. You've heard about this Jesus. The extraordinary, loving miracle-worker. "Take me to him," you say. Someone puts an arm under your arm and leads you to him. What feelings are going on inside you as you walk? *(pause)*

Now you are in the presence of Jesus. He is really and truly present to you at this moment. Feel the sense of privilege to be here. Tell him about your own blindness... (pause)

'Come out of the village,' he says – 'If you want to be able to see, you have to move away from temptation and from the thinking you're used to. Can you put your hand in the hand of Jesus now and allow him to lead you to a different place... How do you feel as he leads you away...? (pause)

Led him rub the spittle on your blindness, and join him in prayer as he prays for you with great love. Sense how much he loves you as he prays... (pause) Pray for healing so that you may no longer be blind but may see Jesus in your family and in your friends and in everyone you meet (pause)

Now you begin to see, but it's blurred. Changing the way you see things is going to take time. Ask Jesus to touch you again and again so that you will be able to see with eyes of faith and love... (pause)

Now Jesus lays his hands on your eyes again, and you begin to see more clearly. And what do you see – you find yourself looking straight at Jesus himself, who loves you more than you can imagine. Talk to him in your own words and say to him whatever you want to say to him... (pause) And now listen to what he wants to say to you... (pause)

Finally, Jesus says, "Do not return to the village." He's asking you not to go backwards. Not to go back to the blindness, to the way of looking at things you were used to. You may like to talk with him about that. (pause) You can open your eyes now and come back in your own time to the room we're in...

JESUS CALMS THE STORM
(Matthew 8 23-27) Philippines version

And when he got into the boat, his disciples followed him. A gale arose on the lake, so great that the boat was being swamped by the waves; but he was asleep. And they went and woke him up saying, 'Lord, save us! We are perishing!' And he said to them, 'Why are you afraid, you of little faith?' Then he got up and rebuked the winds and the sea; and there was a dead calm. They were amazed, saying, 'What sort of man is this, that even the winds and the sea obey him?'

Let's start at the beginning, bearing in mind that the stories in the Bible have always got deep layers of meaning when we remember that Jesus is present here and now, working the same miracles of grace in us as in the story. *And when he got into the boat, his disciples followed him.* Can you see the beautiful lake of Galilee in your mind's eye, with the mountains rising up behind in the distance... (pause) Can you see the sky? What sounds can you hear? Now see Jesus walking down to where the boat is tied. He's looking a bit tired – no wonder, because everybody wants a bit of him, and he had got up this morning before dawn to pray. (pause) The disciples climb into the boat behind him - you're welcome to get in with them too. And the boat pushes out to sea. Jesus stretches out in the back of the boat and falls asleep quickly. Look at the peace of his sleeping face, and let some of his peace and trust in God into your own heart (15 secs)

I'll read the next section: *A gale arose on the lake, so great that the boat was being swamped by the waves; but he was asleep. And they went and woke him up saying, 'Lord, save us! We are perishing!'* This may be a good time to ask yourself, "What's my storm? For some of us, our whole lives are a storm – we're always chasing our tails, behind with things, too much on our plate, feeling we can't cope, living chaotic lives. We could easily say with the disciples, Lord, help us – we are perishing." So what is it that worries me, or frightens me or upsets me? Maybe you're worried about exams coming up, or it may be something that you'd find it hard to talk to anyone about, or it may be some difficulty about friends that's upsetting you. Ask the Holy Spirit to help you see what the storm in *your* life is...? (pause for 30 seconds) So often, when we meet a problem, we're like the disciples: we panic. We forget to have faith in God, to trust that we are in God's hands. So turn to Jesus now – remember that he is as truly present to you at this moment as when he was with the disciples that day in the boat... Bring your fears to him. Don't keep them to yourself. (20secs) And don't be afraid to tell him how weak you are: you might repeat a number of times like the disciples, "Lord, save us! We are perishing!" (20 secs)

And he said to them, 'Why are you afraid, you of little faith?' Then he got up and rebuked the winds and the sea; and there was a dead calm.

Listen to what Jesus says to you: "Why are you so afraid, you of little faith? Why don't you trust me more? Why don't you turn to me instead of trying to deal with your worries and problems on your own..." Let Jesus talk to you... (15 secs) And hand over your fears and worries now into God's hands – let Jesus calm the storm inside you... (20 secs)

They were amazed, saying, 'What sort of man is this, that even the winds and the sea obey him?' Let yourself feel some of their astonishment and wonder. Like them, you are in the loving presence of God who created the world. (pause) And thank God for the hope and the love and the peace of God's Holy Spirit. (pause) When you're ready you can come back gently to the room we're in, and open your eyes...

RAISING OF THE WIDOW'S SON
(Luke 7, 11-17)

Soon afterwards he went to a town called Nain and his disciples and a large crowd went with him. As he approached the gate of the town, a man who had died was being carried out. He was his mother's only son and she was a widow; and with her was a large crowd from the town. When the Lord saw her, he had compassion for her and said to her, "Do not weep." Then he came up and touched the bier and the bearers stood still. And he said, "Young man, I say to you, rise." The dead man sat up and began to speak, and Jesus gave him to his mother. Fear seized all of them and they glorified God, saying, "A great prophet has appeared among us!" and "God has looked favourably on his people." This word about him spread throughout Judea and all the surrounding country.

66

Let's start at the beginning, bearing in mind that the stories in the Bible have always got deep layers of meaning when we remember that Jesus is present here and now, working the same miracles of grace in us as in the story. *Soon afterwards he went to a town called Nain and his disciples and a large crowd went with him.* Can you imagine the scene as a great number of people approach the gates of the town along a dusty road... (10 secs) They're following him in such big numbers because they're attracted to this man who speaks differently to anyone they've ever heard before, and cares about poor people that no one else seems to care much about... See if you can sense the excitement in the people... (10 secs) Now, let's zero in on Jesus himself. Dusty.. thoughtful.. with a lot of warmth in his face and in his eyes. (10 secs) You may like to join the crowd up close to Jesus and watch what happens for yourself. (5 secs)

I'll read the next section: *As he approached the gate of the town, a man who had died was being carried out. He was his mother's only son and she was a widow; and with her was a large crowd from the town.* Can you pick out the mother now and see her tears and her grief. She's a widow. She has already lost her husband, and now her only son. She has no family left, and in those days a widow with no sons had to beg. But she has also lost her nearest and dearest, so she's devastated. And the gospel says there was a large crowd of townspeople – they were grieving with her, shocked by the death of a young man in his prime. See if you can feel a little of the sadness and hopelessness of the scene... (10 secs)

When the Lord saw her, he had compassion for her and said to her, "Do not weep." Then he came up and touched the bier and the bearers stood still. And he said, "Young man, I say to you, rise." Jesus was never interested in performing a miracle to impress people – notice what the passage says, "The Lord had *compassion* for her." Look at his face, see the tenderness and love there. (about 5 seconds) See him touching the stretcher... And the men carrying the stretcher stop and are astonished to hear him say with confidence and authority in his voice, "Young man, I say to you, rise." (about 5 secs)

And we continue with the passage, *The dead man sat up and began to speak, and Jesus gave him to his mother. Fear seized all of them and they glorified God, saying, "A great prophet has appeared among us!" and "God has looked favourably on his people." This word about him spread throughout Judea and all the surrounding country.* Can you see

67

the young man rising from his stretcher? And the astonishment and delight of the crowd, especially the mother – remember that it was for her that Jesus worked this miracle. Can you see the delight and new hope and joy in her face as she hugs her son...? And then the people did what we sometimes forget to do when we have been blessed – they praised and glorified God. (10 seconds)

Jesus is present with us now at this moment. He has the same love and understanding and pity for us, and all those we care for, as he had for the widow. He can see the deadness in us and he wants to offer us hope and new life just as he did then. Let him speak to you now – see the compassion and love in his eyes. (10 seconds) He puts his hands on you and says, '(John/Sarah – say your child's name), I say to you, rise." What does he mean? Let him tell you himself. (about 15 seconds)

Jesus wants to bring healing and new life and hope to you and all your friends and your family. Let's take a few moments to pray for them, remembering that we're praying together in Jesus' name, and our prayers are therefore very powerful and healing for others. (15 seconds)

As usual when we come towards the end of a time of prayer, it's important to thank God for the hope and the love and the new life that God has just given to us and to the people we prayed for, whether we were aware of it or not, so we'll take a moment to be thankful... (Pause) And when you're ready you can come back gently to the room we're in, and open your eyes...

CALLING THE DISCIPLES
(Mark, 1 16-18)

Most of us have our heroes. If we can, we go to hear them speak or we watch a TV programme about them. We read anything written about them in magazines. Their life fascinates us. We follow them closely and even want to be more like them. It's not always pop-stars or footballers or people in the media, though. It may be a teacher or a coach, a priest, a neighbour, a grandparent or an aunt, or a friend of the family. It just happens that there are some people in life who make you feel special and you like being with them. Maybe they're laid back and easy-going. Or they may be quite serious people, but you feel good when you're with them because you know they've time for you and they like you, the vibes are good. Or you like them because they're so genuine and real – and sort of 'together' in themselves. So you like to spend time in their company. And because you're open to them, you usually learn more from them than from anyone else. Which makes you a disciple. Disciples are just people who learn from someone else because of the deep respect they have for that person.

If you had lived at the time of Jesus, you might very well have found him to be a person you had deep respect like that for. Attractive. Fascinating. Warm. Relaxing. Time for you. Someone you love to meet, and to listen to with extra interest. Even to follow.

And the wonderful thing is that when the gospel is read, we meet, not just a person who lived long ago – we actually meet Jesus, really and truly present here and now. That is what Christians believe about the Scriptures, and it is also the experience of those who pray with Scripture. So let's try that with the call of the disciples.

As Jesus passed along the Sea of Galilee, he saw Simon and his brother Andrew casting a net into the lake – for they were fishermen. And Jesus said to them, "Follow me and I will make you fish for people." And immediately they left their nets and followed him.

We'll take it now, one section at a time. *As Jesus passed along the Sea of Galilee, he saw Simon and his brother Andrew casting a net into the lake – for they were fishermen.* See if you can put yourself into the scene. Sit on a stone near the water and look at the blue sky. It's nice and warm. The sun is glinting on a great freshwater lake, so big that it's called a sea. There are mountains beyond the water. And fishermen a little bit out lowering their nets into the water – can you see them? It's the kind of scene a painter might love to paint. Relax and enjoy it... (10 secs)

Now a lone figure appears in the distance. It's the person everyone has been talking about – the one who heals people, who cares for the poor, who speaks with authority... As you watch him come closer, you feel a great reverence and a sense of privilege to be in his presence... (10 secs)

The next line is: *And Jesus said to them, "Follow me and I will make you fish for people." And immediately they left their nets and followed him.* Jesus stops near to where the boat is. The men pause from their work. They've heard the stories about this man. How amazing he is. Different from anyone else. Then they can hardly believe their ears. He's asking them to join him, to follow him. This

69

is crazy. People who work with animals or fish are considered uncouth and sinful at the time. And here he is asking *them* to join him, to follow him. Them!

People in a family business usually have their heads well screwed on: they don't easily drop everything and go off after a wandering preacher. But Simon and Andrew have no hesitation: this guy is different. They don't have to think about it. They feel privileged to be chosen. And they follow him.

But now comes the crunch. What happened in the gospels is happening again here and now. As we read this scene, Jesus becomes truly present with us. He turns around from Simon and Andrew and comes towards where you are sitting on the stone. You stand up, unsure of yourself. He looks at you with eyes that are fascinating, deep, warm. His face has great dignity. Can you see it...? (10 secs) Now he asks the same question of you – will you also become one of my disciples and follow me? Think about it before you answer, because it's not easy to drop your nets and decide, "This is it. This is someone I want to follow to the end." Following him will mean listening to what he says, not acting on my feelings, but stopping and asking him, "What's the most loving thing to do here, Jesus?" Talk for a minute or two with Jesus, tell him your difficulty with what he's asking. And then tell him your decision. (20 secs)

Whatever you've decided, don't worry. Jesus accepts you just as you are. He offers: he doesn't push. It's hard for us to take in that he is such a loving, extraordinary person that he loves us just as much whether we decide to follow him or not. So take a moment to thank him now as we finish our meditation. (10 secs)

A meditation like this is not long enough to deal with the invitation to be a disciple. So you may like to take some time in the next few days to talk further with Jesus about your fears and what holds you back from being a disciple – maybe at night before you fall asleep. Remember, you can pray anytime. When you're ready now, you can open your eyes and come back gently to the room...

HEALING THE MAN WITH THE UNCLEAN SPIRIT
Mark 1 23-26

Just then there was in their synagogue a man with an unclean spirit, and he cried out, 'What have you to do with us, Jesus of Nazareth? Have you come to destroy us? I know who you are, the Holy One of God.' But

Jesus rebuked him, saying, 'Be silent, and come out of him!' And the unclean spirit, throwing him into convulsions and crying with a loud voice, came out of him.

Let's take the first section, *Just then there was in their synagogue a man with an unclean spirit.* To meet the Jesus who is present here and now, it usually helps to get in touch with ourselves first. I need to think about the unclean spirit in myself. For there is a kind of unclean spirit in each one of us. It's a spirit that is negative, full of fears. It's the spirit that makes me feel inferior and insecure and makes me dislike myself. And when we hate ourselves and feel insecure, we try to make ourselves important by thinking the worst of others and looking down on other people and being critical of others. We end up hating others when we hate ourselves. So let's take a minute in silence to be humble before God and get in touch with that unclean spirit in ourselves. (30-60 seconds)

And the next line. *And he cried out, 'What have you to do with us, Jesus of Nazareth? Have you come to destroy us? I know who you are, the Holy One of God.* An unclean spirit is very uncomfortable in the presence of love. It fights love. It can't exist side by side with love. It rightly says to Jesus, 'Have you come to destroy us?' So let's come now into the presence of Jesus, burdened by this nasty spirit within us, and ask humbly for help. (10 seconds) Jesus, you are the most loving person who ever walked the earth, you are the Holy One of God. We come humbly before you, burdened by our negative, unloving thoughts. We are in great need of healing so that we can follow you in love and give our lives to you. Have pity on us please... (pause)

And the last line: *But Jesus rebuked him, saying, 'Be silent, and come out of him!' And the unclean spirit, throwing him into convulsions and crying with a loud voice, came out of him.* Look at Jesus now. He is the exact opposite of this nasty spirit within us – humble, loving, full of goodness. (10 seconds) But there is a stern look in his face in the presence of evil. He speaks with authority. He says to that nasty, proud, spiteful spirit in each of us, 'Be silent, and come out of him. Be silent, and come out of her. Stop that negative, critical whispering within, be off with you, let my beloved people alone, let them grow in love.' Let him say that now to the unclean spirit within you (5-10 seconds). You are in the real presence of Jesus now.

Allow that healing presence to touch you, to enter deep into your soul and to melt away your negative, critical spirit (10 seconds)

God often allows an unclean spirit to remain with us to keep us humble, so it may remain with you, but the difference is that you have now been given the grace to *control* that spirit instead of letting it control you. So let's take a moment to join with Jesus in thanking our Father for healing us. For there has been a real healing of spirit for us, whether we were aware of it or not. (5-10 seconds) Dear God, you are Father and Mother of us all, and you love us more than we can imagine. With Jesus and through Jesus we thank you for the power to overcome the unclean spirit within us. Amen. (pause) And when you're ready you can come back gently to the room we're in...

JESUS COMES TO SIMON'S HOME
(Mark 1, 29-31

As soon as they left the synagogue, they entered the house of Simon and Andrew, with James and John. Now, Simon's mother-in-law was in bed with a fever, and they told him about her at once. He came and took her by the hand, and lifted her up. Then the fever left her, and she began to serve them.

We'll begin with the first section. *As soon as they left the synagogue, they entered the house of Simon and Andrew, with James and John.* Can you imagine how Simon and Andrew felt? They had just left their nets to follow this extraordinary person, Jesus – and now he comes to stay in their home. (pause) How would you feel if you could have Jesus come to stay in this house? (pause) And you can. When you welcome a visitor, a neighbour, a school friend, a relative into your home, you welcome Jesus. Or if you do any act of kindness, a chore for someone in your home, or take time to listen and chat to another member of your family, you are welcoming Jesus into your home. Take a moment to thank him for that privilege and to ask for greater faith, the eyes to see him in others. (10 seconds)

And the next line. *Now, Simon's mother-in-law was in bed with a fever, and they told him about her at once.* This is the lovely thing about welcoming Jesus in your home – you always get more than you give. His is a healing presence, and when you are open to him you too will be healed. But you don't have to be physically ill to be healed. We need healing in all sorts of ways, so let Jesus come to you now as he came to Simon's mother-in-law. He sits down beside you, present to you, interested in you. Can you sense his presence? (pause) Now he asks you what healing you need. Do you need to be healed of your difficulty in forgiving someone, or a habit of showing off, or saying nasty things to someone, or about someone. Tell Jesus in your own words about your difficulty. If you ask for his healing, you will certainly get it. Take your time to talk with him. (20 seconds)

He came and took her by the hand, and lifted her up. Then the fever left her, and she began to serve them. Let Jesus take you by the hand too, and lift *you* up. (pause) Sense the healing in his touch and let him tell you how he is healing you. (10 seconds) But notice something important here – 'then the fever left her, and she began to *serve* them.' Jesus heals us because he loves us – no strings attached – but the real healing and strength comes when we serve others. That's when your healing becomes true healing. So maybe you'd like to make some resolution now to move out of yourself and think of the needs of someone else. Decide what you'll do. (10 seconds) And you might end by taking a moment to thank Jesus in your own words. (10 seconds) And when you're ready you can open your eyes and come back gently to the room we're in...

JESUS CLEANSES A LEPER
(Mark 1, 40-42)

We pray to meet Jesus now as St Mark describes how he healed a leper. *A leper came to him begging him, and kneeling he said to him, 'If you choose, you can make me clean.' Moved with pity, Jesus stretched out his hand and touched him and said to him, 'I do choose. Be made clean!' Immediately the leprosy left him and he was made clean.*

Let's take it a little at a time. *A leper came to him begging him, and kneeling he said to him, 'If you choose, you can make me clean.'* This story isn't just about a leper who lived two thousand years ago. Leprosy in the Bible is a symbol for sin, and we are all sinners – we are all people who sin in the way we treat others or think about others or talk about others – that is our leprosy before God. So let's begin by asking God to help us see the ways *we* suffer from the leprosy of sin in how we fail to respect others... (10 seconds)

And we'll think now about what it's like to be a leper. We can easily overlook the fact that this leper would have been a normal

73

person before he picked up the disease. He may have been a popular person in his village. He may have been deeply loved by his wife and children. But as soon as he was diagnosed, there wasn't even a chance to say goodbye, he had to go immediately and live as an outcast. And that is also what sin does – it cuts us off, makes us outcasts and condemns us like lepers to a hopeless fate. So let's pray for the grace to know how awful sin is (10 seconds)

Yet this leper had one desperate hope left. He had heard of Jesus as a healer, so he went to meet him. And he had great faith, 'If you choose,' he said, ' you can make me clean.' (brief pause) You might like to kneel alongside the leper now as he meets Jesus. (brief pause) And with the leper ask Jesus for his help, perhaps asking with the same words, 'If you choose, you can make me clean.' (10 seconds.)

Now the next line. Moved with pity, Jesus stretched out his hand and touched him and said to him, 'I do choose. Be made clean!' Immediately the leprosy left him and he was made clean.

'Moved with pity.' See the compassion and sadness in Jesus' eyes as he looks at the poor man and understands his pain and isolation… (5 seconds) And now let him turn his eyes to you with the same compassion and understanding.. (5 seconds) And let him say to you, 'I do choose. Be made clean!' (5 seconds) You are in the presence of Jesus now – it is not just your imagination. He is truly present, healing you. Let his warmth and healing and forgiveness spread through your body, forgiving you for the disrespect you have shown others in your thoughts and words and actions. (10 seconds) Part of any healing from sin is to turn over a new leaf and resolve not to sin again, so take a moment for that and to ask for that grace. (pause) Be at peace now and thank Jesus for his love and caring for yourself and for everyone in need. (10 secs) And when you're ready you can come back gently to the room we're in and open your eyes…

A RITUAL MEAL AT HOME

Praying on the Scripture passages above can help a family to begin to experience the presence of Jesus in the first part of the Mass. A ritual meal can be a good way to help children understand what happens in the second half of the Mass. Indeed, Tad Guzie, in his book, *Jesus and the Eucharist* states that "religious educators have found that if they can talk people into making one meal a week a real family meal, a ritual meal with a blessing and a sharing of thanks, and a cup passed around the table, teaching about the Eucharist becomes easy sailing." Below is an outline that may help to introduce that.

Checklist: A glass of water and a bowl, a glass of wine, a tissue, a twig or thin stick, a small fresh roll of French bread on a plate.

We sometimes hear of people who are willing to give their life for others. We usually think that means to die for them. But it doesn't usually mean that. Giving your life for others is what a lot of parents do – they give their time and money and energy day in and day out and wear themselves out for their families. That's giving your life for others. That's what Jesus asks us to do for others.

That's what he did. At the Last Supper, he could have lifted a small stick and said, 'Do you see this stick. It's my body, and look' (breaking it in small pieces) 'it's going to be broken and given up for all the people I love. Take a piece each to keep in memory of me.' And he could have taken water and said, 'Look. Do you see this water? This is my blood that's going to be spilled for you. (spilling the water into a bowl to illustrate). And when I say *Do this in memory of me,* what I'm really asking you is to be willing to do the same as me – to give your life for others.

But Jesus went further. He didn't take water and a piece of wood. First he took a loaf of the ordinary bread at the time. He said, 'Look, do you see this. This is my body.' He broke it as a sign that he was giving his life for us. (breaking it) But then he handed it out and said, "Eat it. I'm giving my life to you now – you will be my Body in future. And this bread will strengthen you and make you able to give your life away like me." (giving it out.)

Then he took the fruit of the grape, which is much richer than water, and he said, 'This is my blood that's going to be spilled for you.' But he didn't spill it into a bowl. He gave it to them and said, "Drink this. I'm giving my life to you now – you will be my Body and Blood in future. It will strengthen you and make you able to love like me." (Passing it around with a tissue.)

What you have just eaten and drunk, of course, is ordinary bread and grape juice. Doing what we have just done may help us to understand better what Jesus was doing, but it's obviously not the same as joining people for Communion at Mass. That's why we went to Mass today as well as doing this.

RESOURCES

BOOKS

There is a series of booklets for parents published by Veritas entitled: **Will our children be okay?** Each one costs around £4-5 stg/€6-7. The titles and authors are: **Will our Children Believe?** by Michael Paul Gallagher SJ **Will our Children have Family Prayer?** by Clare Maloney **How will our Children Grow?** by Christy Kenneally **Your Child and Drugs** by Sean Cassin **Children Feeling Good** by Tony Humphreys **Will our Children Build Healthy Relationships?** by Angela McNamara **Helping your Child through Bereavement** by Mary Paula Walsh **When Parents Separate: Helping your Children Cope** by John Sharry, Peter Reid and Eugene Donohue **Bringing up Responsible Children** by John Sharry **Bringing up Responsible Teenagers** by John Sharry. Or see www.veritas.ie

Enjoy Praying, by Michael and Terri Quinn is a simple introduction to meeting and getting to know Jesus as you pray with Scripture. Available from Family Caring Trust, 8 Ashtree Enterprise Park, Newry, Co. Down BT34 1BY (£7.95/€10.80, incl. post and packing.) Books on parenting by Michael and Terri (each the same price as above) include '**From Pram to Primary School,**' '**What can a Parent do?**' '**What can the parent of a teenager do?**' **Parenting and Sex'** and '**Being Assertive.'** For books and ideas on parenting see www.familycaring.co.uk

Any book by parent and educator Dr Kathleen O'Connell Chesto tends to be simple and fresh and up to date in helping us see the sacred in the ordinary. A good example is **Raising Kids Who Care**, published Sheed and Ward, ISBN 1 55612 921 1. Also **At home with our faith.** And **Growing faith, growing family.**

A book that may be helpful in getting to know the real Jesus is **Jesus before Christianity** (Orbis), by Albert Nolan, ISBN 1570754047.

WEBSITES

www.homefaith.com – practical ideas to develop family spirituality.
www.couples-place.com and www.marriagetools.com sites dedicated to marriage and building relationships.
www.screenit.com – media reviews of latest films and videos

MAKING AGREEMENTS

At the beginning of a course, it can help to discuss and agree on
the following guidelines – or any other concerns you may have.

Play your part. Some people are naturally shy and reluctant to
speak, even in a small group, so no one at any stage *has* to talk in
the group. That said, the more you can take part the better –
talking things out can help the others as well as yourself.

Give the others a chance. If you talk too much, you may spoil
things for others. Please don't speak a second time about a topic
until others have at least had a chance to speak once. Better still if
you can encourage others to talk first. If you practise listening in
the group, you can become a better listener at home too.

What works for you. This programme is to help you to think and
plan for yourself, so you are not expected to use or to agree with
everything in it – we are all different. But you are asked to give
new ideas a fair chance by trying them out.

Keep it to yourself. It is important not to talk outside the group
about anything that is said in the group – things can sound quite
different when they are spoken about out of context.

What works for others. Please do not offer anyone advice.
People have a right to their own approach and their own opinion.
What works for you may not work for them, so feel free to say
what works for you, but it is just not helpful to tell others in the
group what you think *they* ought to do. In the same spirit of
respect, the group leaders will not offer advice either.

Look out for strengths. This is a positive, family-building
support group, so please do not use the group to criticise your
children or others. In any case, it is a basic principle of the course
that to be effective we need to begin by changing *ourselves*.
Others in the family can begin to change when we do.